YOUR LIFE MANUAL

PRACTICAL STEPS TO GENUINE HAPPINESS

Wishing you happiness!

DAVID AMBROSE

David Ambrose

JIMP

**REVOLUTION MIND
PUBLISHING**
CALGARY, ALBERTA
CANADA

www.YourLifeManual.com
www.RevolutionMind.com

Library and Archives Canada Cataloguing in Publication

Ambrose, David, 1950-
Your life manual : practical steps to genuine happiness /
David Ambrose.

Includes bibliographical references and index.
ISBN 0-9739362-0-7

1. Happiness. 2. Self-actualization (Psychology). I. Title.

BF575.H27A42 2006   158.1   C2005-906390-4

ISBN-10: 0-9739362-0-7
ISBN-13: 978-0-9739362-0-9

The extracts and quotations describing *Ubuntu* are from "God Has A Dream" by Desmond Tutu, © 2004, published by Doubleday.

The "Feel Bad, So Distract" diagrams are adapted with permission from the book "The Secret Language of Feelings" by Calvin D. Banyan, © 2003, published by Banyan Publishing, Inc.

"The Station" was originally published in "A Penny's Worth of Minced Ham" by Robert Hastings. © 1986 by the Board of Trustees, Southern Illinois University, reproduced by permission of the publisher.

Cover Design: Peri Poloni-Gabriel, Knockout Design.
www.knockoutbooks.com.
Interior: David Ambrose, Revolution Mind Publishing.
www.RevolutionMind.com
Front Cover Photo: Corbis Images. www. pro.corbis.com
Author Photo: Mathieson & Hewitt Photographers, Calgary.
www.mhphoto.com.

Revolution Mind Publishing
Box 51113 Beddington R.P.O.
Calgary AB T3K 3V0 Canada

info@RevolutionMind.com
www.RevolutionMind.com — www.YourLifeManual.com

Printed and bound in Canada

DEDICATION

To Melanie:
My friend, my love,
my wife, my life.

Your love, encouragement and support
through good times and bad
Lifts me each day.

Disclaimer

This book includes information gleaned from many sources, combined during the author's studies and experiences. This is not intended to be a comprehensive all encompassing philosophical or self-improvement text.

Furthermore, this book is intended to complement and supplement existing literature, not to substitute for independent study and validation by the reader. It is presented to assist people who wish to improve their own lives, although the contents may not be appropriate for all readers. Nothing in this book is intended as a replacement for professional medical or psychological treatment. Particularly, individuals with any history of mental illness or psychological disability should defer to the advice of their treating professional before using any material in this book. There is no intention or desire to diagnose or treat any ailment here.

This book is sold with the understanding that the author and the publisher are not engaged in rendering legal, psychological, accounting or any other professional advice.

Every effort has been made to make this book as complete as possible given the nature of the topic. Much of this book contains information based on experiences of the author, who does not claim that each article of information has been empirically studied or proven. Doing so would preclude sharing this valuable information.

This book is for educational purposes only. The author and publisher shall have no personal liability or responsibility to any person or entity with respect to any loss or damage caused, or alleged to be caused directly or indirectly by the information contained in this book. Any slights of people, places, publishers, books, or organizations are unintentional.

Above all else, look after yourself. Do not do anything that you feel uncomfortable about. Your emotional, spiritual, and physical health must be your prime concern in all that you do.

If you do not wish to be bound by the above, you may return this book in original condition to the publisher for a full refund.

ACKNOWLEDGEMENTS

Much of this book is influenced by the writing and teaching of the Prophets, Masters, and Philosophers who have been guiding and advising us since history began.

Sadly much of their influence on *this* work has gone into the melting pot of my mind and I am unable to accurately allocate credit to each. My thanks to all these visionaries; with the sad observation that humankind still has to learn how to live in peace.

This book would not have been possible without the influence of my father, Roland (Tink) Ambrose. He encouraged an enquiring mind.

I acknowledge too all the people who have shared parts of their lives with me, either as part of my volunteer counseling, or during my hypnotherapy practice. It often seems that those with the most reason to complain, see the really important things more clearly than the rest of us.

Thanks also to family and friends who, over the past thirty-five years or so, have felt safe enough to entrust me with details of their secrets and sorrows.

And thank you to: My editor, Roxane Christ for her eagle eye; Melanie Ambrose (the better half of this family) for her proofing and suggestions; Peri Poloni-Gabriel for the cover design; and last but not least, Calvin Banyan for his support and willingness to impart wisdom.

Editorial Note: Writing presents a problem today when using the personal pronoun (he, she, his, hers, etc.). In modern English, there are no correct gender-neutral alternatives. In this book, I follow the example I first encountered in a book by Calvin Banyan in which he chose to use the feminine unless the reference is specifically masculine. This avoids the use of a stilted "he or she," "her/him," or some other unfamiliar terminology. It also serves, in a small way, to redress the imbalance seen in books through the ages that have ignored the feminine personal pronoun. So where you see the feminine, it could just as easily have been the masculine and it should be understood that way.

Contents

THE STATION
by Robert Hastings

Tucked away in our subconscious minds is an idyllic vision in which we see ourselves on a long journey that spans an entire continent. We're traveling by train and, from the windows, we drink in the passing scenes of cars on nearby highways, of children waving at crossings, of cattle grazing in distant pastures, of smoke pouring from power plants, of row upon row of cotton and corn and wheat, of flatlands and valleys, of city skylines and village halls.

But uppermost in our minds is our final destination—for at a certain hour and on a given day, our train will finally pull into the station with bells ringing, flags waving, and bands playing. And once that day comes, so many wonderful dreams will come true. So restlessly, we pace the aisles and count the miles, peering ahead, waiting, waiting, waiting for the station.

"Yes, when we reach the station, that will be it!" we promise ourselves. "When we're eighteen ... win that promotion ... put the last kid through college ... buy that 450 SL Mercedes Benz ... pay off the mortgage ... have a nest egg for retirement."

From that day on we will live happily ever after.

Sooner or later, however, we must realize that there is no station in this life, no one earthly place to arrive at once and for all. The journey is the joy. The station is an illusion—it constantly outdistances us. Yesterday's a memory, tomorrow's a dream. Yesterday belongs to history, tomorrow belongs to God. Yesterday's

11

a fading sunset, tomorrow's a faint sunrise. Only today is there light enough to love and live.

So, gently close the door on yesterday and throw the key away. It isn't the burdens of today that drive men mad, but rather the regret over yesterday and the fear of tomorrow.

"Relish the moment" is a good motto, especially when coupled with Psalm 118:24, "This is the day which the Lord hath made; we will rejoice and be glad in it."

So stop pacing the aisles and counting the miles. Instead, swim more rivers, climb more mountains, kiss more babies, count more stars. Laugh more and cry less. Go barefoot oftener. Eat more ice cream. Ride more merry-go-rounds. Watch more sunsets. Life must be lived as we go along.

Originally published in "A Penny's Worth of Minced Ham" by Robert Hastings. © 1986 by the Board of Trustees, Southern Illinois University, reproduced by permission of the publisher.

FOREWORD

What is genuine happiness? Could such a thing truly exist? If it does, dare we ask it to last more than a fleeting moment, an hour or a day? Are some people just lucky to have been born into a life where happiness can be found, or are some people fortunately born with a happiness gene, and as a result seemingly happier than others?

What about love, peace, freedom and harmony? Are they just hollow words only meaningful to poets, and dreamers? Are they ideals that we can truly work toward?

Or, are there things that a person can do to change how she feels? Are there steps that can be taken to change ones own experience in life that can bring much more of these wonderful things into ones own experience in a predictable way?

So many questions! You hold in your hand a step-by-step manual containing steps that you can really take to increase your own happiness, while increasing the amount of love, peace, freedom and harmony that you can experience in your life, while at the same time generating it out into the world.

In this book, *Your Life Manual: Practical Steps to Genuine Happiness*, David Ambrose does a beautiful job of giving you what you have always wanted, a roadmap to a more fulfilling and happy life. You deserve this gift! But don't just read this book; take the time to use it. Really go through the process that David provides for you, and you will find that these steps can really make a difference in your life. You will also find that as you bring more happiness into your life you will also bring more happiness into the lives of those you love and care about.

In this book, you will not only learn how to become happier, and live a more fulfilling life, but you will learn how to be grateful for even those painful moments in your life, past, present and future. You will learn that all feelings are good and those emotions, be they pleasurable or painful, are really a God given (or nature given, if you prefer) internal guidance system, a system which reveals your own inner wisdom, so often ignored in modern society. Learn how anger, sadness, loneliness and other painful emotions are really signs on the roadway of your life, coming from deep within you, guiding you to genuine happiness.

As you read this book, you will learn about how certain principles are always working in your life, and as you learn about them you will learn that they are "laws" that once understood, place you into a natural flow toward a more fulfilling life.

I urge you to read and use this book as it was meant to be used, as a multi-phased approach to changing your life, through learning time-tested principles, and implementing them into your life, so that you can find genuine happiness.

Calvin D. Banyan, MA
Board Certified Hypnotherapist
Creator of the 5-PATH™ Hypnotherapy
and 7th Path Self-Hypnosis® Systems
Author of, The Secret Language of Feelings
www.CalBanyan.com

PREFACE

We all want to be happy. It is one thing to be happy; it is another to be genuinely happy. We have all experienced happiness when something good or nice happens, but this happiness is transitory; the joy of it soon passes.

Genuine happiness, on the other hand, does not require frequent injections of good fortune. It is the state of mind that we occupy where we are content with ourselves and with our surroundings.

Reaching this state of mind is not difficult, you don't have to become a hermit, climb a mountain to sit in solitude for years on end. Although it is not difficult, getting there requires that we create a foundation (a basic philosophy coupled with a code of principles) reflecting our identity—a set of "truths" that we accept after due contemplation to guide us through whatever should transpire, whether favorable or unfavorable.

Happiness without this groundwork can be compared to a house built without a proper foundation: chances are it will endure the trials of time, but the chances are quite slim. Unlike building a house though, it is never too late to build or reinforce the foundation of your life.

Whatever your foundation is (or isn't), will directly affect your future and how happy your life is.

Once this foundation is in place and (at least preliminary) principles have been adopted, we have a basis for the daily

decisions and choices that we are called upon to make throughout our lives. Our philosophy and principles help to guide us
through life on our own terms.

You can determine how genuinely happy you are.

Introduction

Imagine living the rest of your life happy—not smiling or grinning all day long, but enjoying the contented feeling that comes from knowing who you are. Not only do you know who you are, but you are happy with the person you are and are comfortable with your place in this crazy world.

You are free of all the negative, self-defeating feelings and insecurities that have ever plagued you. Undue anger and resentment, guilt and anguish are all history.

Life does not always run smoothly (and never will), but you are so much better at calming the waters when they get rough or at riding out the storms; whichever is most appropriate to the situation.

Your past does not hold you back, your present is an adventure, and your future is full of infinite and exciting possibilities.

Like that picture? You can have it. It will take a little effort on your part, but the good news is that there is no exam! It is easier than school, and you *can* do it!

As you are reading, I obviously have no idea who you are or even where you are. I don't know you, but I do know some things about you.

I *do* know that you are exactly where you should be. There is nowhere else you could possibly be, which is not exactly where you are meant to be at that precise moment.

I also know that you are a truly unique, wonderful, and special human being. You have unique talents and abilities to offer the world. It may be that (with a little help from your family or friends) you have convinced yourself that you are not all of these things.

But you are. This is one thing I know for sure!

I also assume there is a level of contentment you wish to reach, that has eluded you until now.

I hope this book will help you achieve the happiness and contentment you desire. The message contained in these pages is not especially new—in fact, much of what follows is based on ideas and opinions that have been around for thousands of years; the teaching of the sages of our history.

Included here, are concepts, thoughts, ideas and conclusions that have helped me reach a level of happiness and contentment I would not have believed possible for an ordinary, somewhat damaged person like me. The discoveries I made changed my life. They can help change yours too.

This is a summary of over half a lifetime of searching and contemplating—looking for answers and reasons, trying to make sense of life. Even though it was a personal journey, just as yours is a personal journey, this is not a book about my journey or about me. There are conclusions and ideas that I believe are universally worthy. Where it seems appropriate, I have included details of personal experiences, but these are provided merely to expand or illustrate a point.

One of the first requirements for me was that it all had to make sense—even if it was a weird unscientific kind of sense. It had to have some undefined *feeling* of possibility.

The Roman Catholic Bible* states that all things are ordered in measure and number and weight. With sufficient study, anything ordered will make sense.

---

* Wisdom 11:21

This book is divided into four distinct sections:

In Part One, the philosophy that evolved from a young teen's search for the ultimate truth is briefly outlined. It is simple, short and idealistic, but has been found worthy by thousands of visitors to the LovePeace.com web site.

Part Two moves forward from the philosophy with a list of practical realizations. These fifteen principles or "truths" are the foundation and building blocks that provide guidance in this chaotic world. Every eventuality cannot be foreseen, so these principles are the beacons we use to maintain direction.

Then, in Part Three, we look at life and explore actual steps that can be taken to help you achieve greater happiness and reach your goals. We look at thought patterns and learned responses. We also describe some of the exercises you can easily use to enhance the positive and outweigh the negative influences of your life; thus attaining your goal of peace and contentment.

In Part Four, we include several essays and ideas, which offer alternative views on various subjects. These further expand on ideas already discussed, or introduce others to provoke thought and consideration.

We will delve into the spiritual, physical, and philosophical worlds. They are really just one anyway. The separation of subjects or points of observation is the work of us humans. We love to categories everything, don't we? Is it possible that our spiritual and secular lives can exist independently? It doesn't seem likely.

Having said that, this is not a book about religion. Whatever your religious or spiritual beliefs may be, you may not agree with some of my ideas; there are undoubtedly other perfectly valid alternatives. The process to achieve the desired result does not change, even if we differ on specific points.

Before diving in, please realize that it is unlikely anyone would be able to incorporate fully all of the ideas and concepts described here into their lives. We are all human, life is a voyage; it is seeking answers and striving for happiness, which leads to joy.

We are each unique, so there is really no such thing as one-size-fits-all—especially when we are dealing with what really makes you, *you*.

As far as possible our philosophy and these principles are applicable, whatever your culture or beliefs are. Only bigots (who will probably not have picked up this book anyway) are likely to find anything offensive. If, however, there is any part that does not gel with your sensibilities, whatever remains should be just as useful to you. Sift through, use what clicks for you, and leave out what doesn't.

Be gentle with yourself. Have fun.

PART ONE

THE PHILOSOPHY

Just for today, do not worry.
Just for today, do not anger.
Honor your parents, teachers and elders.
Earn your living honestly.
Show gratitude to all things

~ *Dr. Mikao Usui*
Developer of Reiki

· 1 ·

A BRIEF BACKGROUND

L ove, Peace, Freedom, Harmony, and Happiness. This sounds like sixties hippie mumbo jumbo, but believe it or not, these concepts also represent the basis for a way of life, which really works and can make you a better, happier, and more confident human being. Adopting these concepts as a way of life will ultimately lead you to play a role in revitalizing the planet as well! As we dig deeper, you'll find that this philosophy, combined with a little common sense, will help provide answers to questions you may have been asking yourself for some time.

A philosophy of life (whatever it is) is necessary to provide direction. You will discover that there is no situation where the consideration of this philosophy will fail to offer the correct solution or course of action required in that circumstance. If you think about it, and practice it—it works.

Allow me some indulgence while I begin, more or less, at the beginning.

The hippie movement of the sixties had a deep impact on thousands (perhaps millions) of people. It particularly affected those who were young at the time, me included. Curiously, many young people, who were born long after it all seemed to have ended, are similarly affected today, nearly half a century later.

The Beatles appeared to change the world when I was eleven, their first single peaking at number 17 on the UK charts, on my twelfth birthday. Between then and the Woodstock "happening" in 1969, when I was eighteen, the boundaries to our minds were dismantled or pushed back forever.

It was a magical time for those of us who were around at that time. Anything and everything was possible.

Stuck on the southern tip of Africa in a narrow minded, repressive and totalitarian society, the effect was even more indelible on my idealistic mind than it was on those living in San Francisco or London. Since this new philosophy was all received second hand, the ideals of love and peace carried more weight than it did for those actually living it—being caught up in the free sex, drugs, and the other perversions that eventually undermined the credibility of the ideal.

The freedom the youth of that generation demanded dealt a devastating blow to the structured way of life our parents knew. We were naïve, for sure. The well-worn slogan "Sex, Drugs, and Rock 'n' Roll," adequately expressed the excesses in which the young people of the sixties reveled.

In the isolated world in which I dwelled, love, peace, and freedom were in a purer form. The ideals were good, but at that stage they were no more than ideals. Now, those of us who survived are all a little older and wiser.

The really weird thing is that I only found out years later that in the Xhosa and Zulu languages they use the word *ubuntu*, (pronounced "oo-boon-to") which more or less encapsulates this philosophy in one word. We will take a closer look at this wonderful concept a little later.

What follows is not a ponderous philosophical treatise—it is a skeleton. Far more important than describing the philosophy, is integrating its principles into our lives. We will get into the specifics of how to do this in later sections.

Now the time is right. Let's go through the components of this philosophy one by one.

· 2 ·

<u>LOVE</u>

Wherever you look for a definition of the word *love*, whether in a dictionary or on the Internet, you will find a vast number of definitions and interpretations of this one little word.

To describe 'love' as expressed in the context of this book, and to differentiate it from other meanings, it is useful for us to look at the different words the ancient Greeks used for this one little English word.

> *Eros*: As you can probably guess from the name, this refers to desire, erotic or sexual love. Romantic love. *Eros* is driven by desire.
>
> *Storge*: Is the kind of love that exists in families – such as the love between a parent and a child. Natural affection. *Storge* is determined by instinct.
>
> *Philia*: The love of friendship and affection—sisterly or brotherly love, rather than romantic. Friendship, platonic love. *Philia* develops through bonding.
>
> *Agape*: Divine or unconditional love. It is a self-sacrificing love that expects nothing in return. It exists even in the face of rejection. In contrast to the other forms of love, *Agape* is given purely by choice.

So the 'love' discussed throughout these pages is *Agape* (pronounced "ah-GAH-peh"). This is the selfless love for all, for nature, our planet, and everything else! This is the love which Jesus preached.

The different forms of love differ significantly when it comes to the object of love. *Eros* love is usually directed at a single person. *Agape* love is directed at the whole of humanity—perhaps everything else too.

This love is many things:

+ It is compassion for all creatures.
+ It is acceptance of what is, and who we are.
+ It embraces our differences and forgives all.
+ It looks for ways to improve the lot of the entire planet.
+ It is not necessary to "like" to love, just as it is not necessary to love to "like."

Looking at the world today, the papers and television, there is not much of this love in evidence. Our society is not attuned to love or concern for the other person. Or is it?

Watching our TV screens we delight in seeing the next person voted out of the latest smash reality series. Not so long ago, we used to cheer for particularly skilled contestants, now we enjoy seeing those who are weaker (or less devious) belittled publicly.

Our sporting heroes are charged with one goal only: Win.

In the old days, the requirement in sport was to do the best that you could; but sportsmanship was paramount. More important than winning, was how you played the game.

Doing your best and being fair is no longer acceptable. Children, of course, have been influenced by this behavior as well, since the requirement (and desire) to win has become essential and has been carried over into their sporting endeavors and school results. It is little wonder that today's youngsters are under the stress levels that they are. Then in business, the desire and requirement to win is continued. Win at all costs.

Whoever dies with the most money wins!

In ancient Greece, in the days of the City States, there was a fearsome enemy of Athens called Sparta. For the Spartans, lying, cheating, stealing, and murdering were all okay, as long as you did not get caught. Being caught was the greatest failure. Looking around can we see signs of this mentality in our corporations? Think Enron.

The concept of caring for your employees is a thing of the past. In my father's day, it was common for people to work for the same company all their working lives—because "if you displayed loyalty they would look after you."

And let's not even get into politics!

The title of the old song 'Love Is All Around' is somewhat off the mark when we look around us at all the places we go and at all the things we do.

Some people would say the world has changed and this is just the way it is. Accept it.

Looking behind the headlines though, there is abundant evidence of ordinary people doing the most extraordinary altruistic deeds to help others. We all know about Mother Teresa of Calcutta – but there are literally thousands of people whose life's work is helping others with little or no reward.

In my native South Africa, we heard of many of these "saints" who struggle to make ends meet, yet devote their lives to the care and support of AIDS orphans, homeless, or other destitute groups discarded by society. These patrons of the poor work quietly in the background, receiving little or no fanfare, and little thanks.

Unfortunately, because of the selfless attitude of these helpers of humanity working away from the public eye, we do not hear about them. We could be excused for assuming they do not exist … but they do, and hearing their stories would enrich our lives.

∾

As humans, our driving desire is to be happy. The best way to feel happy is to love and to be loved. All love is connected, and we feel happiness whether we are experiencing *Eros* love or *Agape* love. In the long run though, the satisfaction of love is greater through *Agape* love.

Agape loves everyone and everything. Whether we like or approve of someone is immaterial. Loving and condoning do not mean the same thing. Indeed, it is perfectly possible to love those who hate you. There are many examples of this in history.

Love is crucial to happiness. Without the giving component of love, any feeling of happiness will be a shallow imitation of true happiness. Giving love makes us happy. It is by giving love that we receive love. Receiving love makes us feel complete.

We can train ourselves to love everyone and everything. It starts with caring. It takes commitment and effort but like everything, it becomes easier with practice.

· 3 ·

PEACE

Universal peace is the goal. Peace is not just the absence of war; it is an awful lot more than that!

Peace is an attitude, a state of mind towards everything around us. For peace to exist, we need to be prepared to resist all forms of violence, with as much fervor as if we were fighting for our survival. We actually are.

The path to peace includes the elimination of all forms of violence—whether physical, verbal, or emotional—in all spheres of life. Anything forced upon another living creature contributes to conflict and violence; it is just the degree that varies.

Sadly, there seems to be aggression and violence everywhere... violent crime, human rights abuses and numerous wars.

It is peculiar that so many wars are fought in the name of justice or religion. Wars are not just; the people who die are, for the most part, the innocent ones. There is disagreement regarding the position of some religions on war, but generally if war or violence is permitted it is only for self-defense, or in defending those oppressed.

In contrast to the manipulating views broadcast by politicians, the media, and anyone else benefiting from war, looking back at the lessons of history the message is clear:

Violence and war do not buy peace.
They only buy violence and war, death and destruction.

One wonders how many wars would have been averted if the leaders and their families had been compelled to take their place amongst the troops at the front lines...

On an interpersonal level, there are conflicts everywhere we look. Sometimes it may be mild rivalry. Other times, words said in anger. Each of these provides fertile ground for escalating hostility and violence if not controlled.

In conflict, whether in personal or international matters, nobody really wins. There may appear to be a winner and a loser, but this loss breeds resentment—as evidenced by continuing terrorist attacks and ongoing feuds. True peace does not result from confrontational exchanges.

∼

Peace has been mistaken for weakness. It is not. Non-violence takes immense courage in the face of a powerful aggressor.

History is peppered with examples of non-violence standing up to aggression and power—one of the most visual being the photograph of the lone man standing up to the might of China, halting the progress of the tanks in Tiananmen Square in 1989.

Our bloody history illustrates that preserving peace is often more difficult than violent retaliation.

Living in peace allows us to reach our full potential. We can train ourselves to live in peace. It begins with accepting that there are alternatives, then renouncing all violence.

· 4 ·

FREEDOM

Freedom is most definitely *not* the right to do whatever you want and to hell with the consequences! That is not freedom, it is anarchy.

Freedom allows us *to choose* how and where we will live. It allows us *to associate* with anyone we wish. Within reason, it allows us *to decide* upon things that affect us, but freedom comes at a price. Freedom has obligations.

You cannot be truly free if you deny freedom to others. Therefore, freedom demands consideration for others. It also requires vigilance; monitoring, watching those who may wish to erode our freedom or the freedom of others.

To ensure our freedom we need to honor everyone else's freedom, and then do what we can to bring freedom to all who are not free—in a non-violent way—wherever they are.

True freedom includes allowing other people freedom of speech, religion, association, politics, sexual preference, or whatever, regardless of our own views or opinions on the matter.

People who strongly believe that they know what is best for the rest of a community (or humanity, for that matter) are sometimes driven to convert others to their way of thinking. This desire to change other people can take many forms. The lengths they will go to in order to achieve their objective is often in direct proportion to the fervor of the feeling or belief.

Unfortunately, as we know from the past, these fanatical opinions can lead to state sponsored discrimination, unfair legislation, murder, mob violence, exile, and various other forms of condemnation. Examples of these blots upon the history of humankind are the Inquisition, Hitler's Holocaust, and South Africa's Apartheid regime. Thankfully these are in the past, but there are others that are ongoing in various parts of the world as you read this.

Some fundamental religious groups and individuals are even prepared to go as far as the murder of sinners and infidels, generating fear to enforce their opinions.

Censorship has been a tool wielded mercilessly by governments desiring to control the population. It is also a device promoted and extolled by radical groups to restrict those who think or act differently.

We naturally have to protect the young and the innocent. Nobody would propose that impressionable children be subjected to experiences that could harm them physically or psychologically—but as adults, we must recognize censorship for what it is. It erodes freedom.

The freedom we offer as a model is really pretty simple. As an adult, you should be free to do whatever you wish...with the single limitation that exercising your freedom must not infringe upon the right of others to love, to live in peace, to exercise freedom and to enjoy harmony and happiness.

· 5 ·

HARMONY

Most definitions of the word *harmony* use words such as agreement, compatibility, and congruity. All of these can occur naturally and spontaneously in human relationships.

We can consider harmony occurring naturally on a wider scale too—the harmony of the universe, the balance of nature.

Where it does not exist ordinarily, promoting or creating harmony can *really* take some work! Yet if we want to live this life of happiness, co-existing in harmony is essential.

With personal interactions, this is probably one of the areas most of us need to concentrate the greatest effort. This is really "live and let live" put in practice.

One of the main causes of conflict on this planet is the inability to apply this concept—especially when confronted with strongly held views, such as religious belief or political affiliation.

To live in harmony, we need to accept that there are other points of view—and be content with this fact. Understanding and accepting that there are other opinions, entitles us to retain our own opinions.

Only allowing the airing of different points of view enables us to determine what is real and what is not. It is always worthwhile to test our position against that of others. This is how we grow as people and become wiser.

Another essential aspect to the attainment of harmony is forgiveness. It can be difficult to let go of an affront. For some reason, some people find it extremely difficult, if not impossible, to either apologize, or to forgive. Why do we hang onto something so negative that it diminishes us?

In the small and large conflicts that we get into throughout our lives, admitting responsibility for the cause of the disagreement will often defuse a potentially explosive situation. *Sorry* is such a small, but powerful word.

From the other side of an argument (if you are not in the wrong), forgiveness is a very powerful tool you can use to empower yourself: to let go of the anger or hurt and regain your harmony and serenity. The process of forgiveness will be discussed later. Learning to forgive has changed lives for the better. It can set you free from negative emotions that have been inhibiting your potential.

Despite what we grow up believing, truth is not as precise as we like to believe. Your truth (belief, point of view) may not be the same as the next person's, and that is okay—it doesn't mean that you are necessarily wrong.

It often helps to try seeing things from the other person's point of view and accepting the validity of that opinion from their standpoint without having to agree with it.

Once again, as we practice getting along with everyone despite differences, it becomes easier.

·6·

HAPPINESS

Ultimately this is what we all want, over anything else. Happiness is something that happens to you as a consequence of what you are doing or have done. It is not something for which you search. It comes to you of its own accord, although you can take steps to reach happiness too.

You can be happy whatever your lot in life. Whether you are living out on the streets or in a mansion, you can be just as happy. Believing that winning the lottery, or getting a better job, or whatever will make a difference to your ability to be happy is a fallacy. Actually, if you are not happy before a windfall, chances are you will be less happy soon after it occurs.

Material happiness is no substitute for real, internal happiness. The happiness resulting from a sudden windfall is transitory. All it does is briefly divert your attention away from those things that prevented you from feeling happy before the windfall*.

Surely it is better to reflect on what we *do* have than on what we *don't* have? Strangely, a lot of people seem to prefer keeping happiness at bay by bemoaning their misfortune at every opportunity. This is a defense mechanism, unconsciously employed to save them from being hurt or disappointed. This attitude manifests when our natural positive outlook on life has been outweighed by negative influences and experiences.

---

*   This diversion of feelings is discussed at some length in later chapters.

There is an enormous amount of negativity around us at all times. It starts when we are children, and unfortunately continues until we die.

We need to use every opportunity to offset the negative energy we've absorbed so far and to fend-off future negativity.

Happiness occurs when you are able to shake off the claws of negativity and admit the positive – when you face the world, with neither guilt, nor fear; when you *feel* whatever emotions arise, without them overwhelming you. Happiness occurs when you strive to attain a goal and see life as an adventure to be lived to the full, whatever that means for you.

Happiness occurs when you hear the music of life!

· 7 ·

UBUNTU

Long before European settlers spread into the area around the southern edge of Africa, a proud nation of black people called the Xhosa lived there.

Because of the clicking sounds of some consonants, the word Xhosa is difficult for Westerners to pronounce, most pronouncing it as *kaw-suh*.

These people were considered to be savages by many of the settlers, but they had a highly developed social structure based on traditional values, which had evolved over thousands of years. The foundation of this structure was embodied in the single word: *ubuntu*—a word with no English equivalent. One definition is: *a person is a person through other persons.*

The South African Nobel Laureate Archbishop Desmond Tutu, an extraordinary man of Xhosa descent, has described the meaning of *ubuntu* in a few of his books.

In *God Has A Dream*, (an excellent book regardless of one's beliefs) he expands upon the meaning, saying:

> ...It is the essence of being human. It speaks of the fact that my humanity is caught up and is inextricably bound up in yours. I am human because I belong. It speaks about wholeness, it speaks about compassion. A person with *ubuntu* is welcoming, hospitable, warm and generous, willing to share. Such

people are open and available to others, willing to be vulnerable, affirming of others, do not feel threatened that others are able and good, for they have a proper self-assurance that comes from knowing that they belong in a greater whole. They know that they are diminished when others are humiliated, diminished when others are oppressed, diminished when others are treated as if they were less than who they are. The quality of *ubuntu* gives people resilience, enabling them to survive and emerge still human despite all efforts to dehumanise them.

More and more, we are discovering that everyone and everything is interconnected. What hurts you hurts me. What heals you heals me.

It is obvious that our attitudes and emotions have an effect on those around us. Similarly, feelings of wellbeing or despair in a group (or community, or nation) permeate through the members of the group.

Sensitive travelers can often notice differences in the mood or "vibe" of the countries or areas they visit.

The consideration of others used to play a much larger part in human interaction in earlier times. In recent times however, human interaction has been based on individual needs, achievements and desires.

This more self-centered approach to life and decision-making has undoubtedly produced more wealth and power for some, but the cost to humanity, the poor, and to the planet has been huge.

According to the United Nations Development Program, more than 1.3 billion people (a quarter of the world's population) live in severe poverty. If each of us earning money were to donate 1% (yes, just one percent!) of our income, world poverty could be eradicated!

As became common knowledge during the Live 8 concerts and the Make Poverty History campaign in 2005, a child dies of extreme poverty every three seconds. All of this is because of a lack of *ubuntu*.

The effect of this self-focusing culture on the overall development of our species will only be ascertained sometime in the future when there is some distance allowing for an unbiased assessment. My expectation is that our time will be seen as a low point on our evolution.

The Spanish Inquisition, seen as good and necessary at the time, but a blot on our past, lasted more than three centuries, and resulted in (probably) no more than a hundred and thirty thousand deaths. Children dying due to poverty will reach that number in *less than five days*!

Times are changing though. In recent years, there has been a growing interest in achieving more balance in life. The personal cost of the "I-me-mine" syndrome is becoming more apparent in its effect on relationships, health, and general well being, not to mention poverty and the environment.

∾

More love, peace, freedom, harmony, happiness, and *ubuntu*, on a large scale, will undoubtedly help to boost the process.

It starts with you and me.

It can be fun and make you happy as you explore that remarkable person you see when you look in the mirror.

You know when ubuntu *is there, and it is obvious when it is absent. It has to do with what it means to be truly human, to know that you are bound up with others in the bundle of life.*

~ Archbishop Desmond Tutu
in "God Has A Dream"

· 8 ·

In A Nutshell

Over the years, what started as an idealistic interpretation of the "Flower Child's Principles" has evolved, becoming a practical philosophy that can be applied to daily life in the 21st Century. It has the potential to change every aspect of our lives and interpersonal relationships fundamentally.

As unrealistic as this may seem to some, adopted by enough people, this philosophy will change the way the world works:

- *Where there is mutual respect for all creatures,*
- *Where the well being of the planet is sacred,*
- *Where the integrity of our leaders is a given, and*
- *Where all who embrace the concepts of Love, Peace, Freedom, Harmony, and Happiness can live by these concepts safely.*

The time is ripe for change.

The best way to start is to change ourselves and then by our example, change those around us. As we begin to incorporate this new outlook and its values into every part of our lives, we let every one of our choices reflect those values.

By doing this, we start a groundswell that builds and compounds until it reaches the point where those who direct our communities will be influenced to incorporate the philosophy into their platforms as well. It will grow slowly, from a local level through to national and international affairs.

But it starts with you and me. We become happier, and change the world in the process.

Although the overall payoff can be huge, for now, focus on yourself as you progress through the following chapters. Focus on the small steps; the giant leaps will follow in their own time.

Worthwhile change seldom just happens. Anyone who has tried to lose weight will tell you! But you really can do whatever you set your mind to do, provided you are prepared to do what it takes while you strive towards your goal.

As mentioned in the introduction, you are a unique, wonderful, and special person. You really do have unique talents and abilities to offer the world.

With dedication and practice, it is merely a matter of time until you transform yourself into the person you truly want to be.

I mean: The person that *YOU* want to be, not the person that your parents, teachers, friends, boss, spouse, or anyone else wants ...*you*.

You will notice small changes quicker than you would have imagined, so expect to notice!

You will be happy.

PART TWO

THE PRINCIPLES: BUILDING THE FOUNDATION

With no solid foundation,
strength and integrity
is soon undermined.

Built upon a strong foundation,
Sound principles guide us
towards fulfilment and happiness.

· 9 ·

Bringing It Down To Earth

In developing the backbone for this way of looking at life, I soon realized that there would have to be a number of key concepts or assumptions to use as a foundation upon which to build. The philosophy we have just described is good, but we really need more practical, down to earth markers to guide us on the journey to happiness.

These basic tenets are naturally very important because they will flavor any conclusions that are drawn in any given circumstance. Luckily, there are thousands of philosophers, teachers, prophets, elders, and other wise people who have pondered these same questions, so it was not necessary to start from scratch.

Even though there is an enormous amount of information available, there are significant differences of opinion depending upon which source or idea is adopted. Never being one to blindly accept anything (this trait is what got me here in the first place!), each building block of this foundation had to be considered carefully before being adopted or modified.

It is possible that you may disagree with some of these ideas, or my interpretations, and that is fine. All I ask, is that you think about them. Consider them and if you disagree, know why.

Even as I write, I realize that this list will grow and change, perhaps even shrink to something more compact and appropriate. Because reality does not generally neatly fit into arbitrary categories, these building blocks overlap to some extent.

Absolute Rights:

The Right to LOVE
The Right to PEACE
The Right to FREEDOM
The Right to HARMONY
The Right to HAPPINESS

· 10 ·

ABSOLUTE RIGHTS

This is perhaps the foundation of the foundation!

All creatures and things have the absolute right to love, peace, freedom, harmony, and happiness. Notice the phrase "all creatures," rather than "all people"—it intentionally includes animals and insects too. Possibly even inanimate objects and plants, although not everyone would want to go that far.

Doesn't it seem a little bigoted to assert that we are superior to all other creatures, in all respects? And if we do consider ourselves superior, should other creatures have no right to be treated with dignity? Are we justified in treating them like … animals?

Adolf Hitler and his followers believed that Jews, gypsies, and others were sub-human; therefore they did not deserve humane treatment and could justly be used in brutal medical experiments, herded like cattle and killed like vermin.

In South Africa and other places, many racists still consider black people to be a step below human.

It is pretty certain that you would not care to be likened to Hitler or be considered a racist; however those same people who supported these atrocities on humanity would vigorously defend their position with some kind of perverted logic that makes sense to them.

As we become more enlightened, we realize that the discriminatory views and laws of the past can no longer be accepted or condoned. Today, the suggestion of women being prevented from voting simply because of their gender is totally unacceptable in any Western democracy; yet it was not that long ago that the very thought of a woman understanding the complexities of government, was laughable.

The point is: We are not the fastest, or the largest, or the strongest creatures on this planet. We do not have the largest brain, we do not live longest, nor can we withstand nature's extremes or nuclear radiation.

And if you think about it, we have not done much good for this planet either. We may be the most advanced intellectually, but shouldn't that make us more responsible and caring of our fellow Earth inhabitants and the planet itself?

The degree to which you accept this principle may not be as broad as suggested here, as long as your acceptance, at least, includes all other humans. It will probably also go as far as including some animals too.

∾

For a long time now, I have had the dream of finding a way to avoid the millions of laws and regulations that are used to govern each country and community.

Eventually, I came upon one that seemed to cover every possible eventuality in one short sentence.

Unfortunately, I later found that this concept is similar to conclusions reached hundreds of years ago by thinkers such as Jeremy Bentham, but the simplicity of this one sentence is pretty neat.

What is nice about it too, is that it is a positive law. By that, I mean it focuses on what *may* be done rather than what may *not* be done:

> *You may do anything that doesn't infringe*
> *upon any one else's rights.*

In our terms, this "universal law" would encompass the rights to love, peace, freedom, harmony, and happiness. And since this law would apply to everyone, everyone else can also do anything that doesn't infringe upon anyone else's rights.

Think about it.

We all know that we must not steal or murder, it is wrong (and against the law). In terms of this single law you mustn't steal or murder because you would be infringing your victim's rights to peace, freedom, harmony, and happiness. That is an easy one.

If you are driving along and you cut in front of a car in the next lane, you are infringing the rights of that driver. You have violated his right to peace, harmony, and probably happiness!

If you reflect on the last time you felt angry or frustrated with another person, you will find they infringed some or all of these rights on one way or another.

By the same token, do you remember the last time someone was upset with you? Can you identify which of their rights you took away from them?

Just as with the laws enacted by our political leaders, there are degrees of severity when it comes to withholding or depriving others of their rights. The subject of crime and punishment is provocatively addressed in Part Four.

*In life
excess in one area,
leads to excess in others.*

*The consequence
of equilibrium,
is harmony.*

· 11 ·

BALANCE IS BEAUTIFUL

In all things, balance is the key. It is likely that the causes of all the problems facing us (the planet and all other inhabitants too, for that matter) can be traced to excesses that have thrown related cycles out of balance.

Our efforts to manipulate nature clearly show this. Extreme deforestation upsets the ecological balance of the area. Deforestation has been shown to change climatic conditions. Effects include temperature increases; soil drying out; decreased recycling of carbon dioxide by plants; and increased erosion. The controversial question of global warming and the greenhouse effect is another example of us upsetting the balance that has protected our atmosphere, and Earth itself, for millennia.

The pharmaceutical industry is very good at developing products aimed at improving one or other aspect of our lives. Whether for relieving pain or depression; increasing or decreasing the chances of conception; eradicating disease; or body sculpting—there seem to be few limits to their expertise. There have been numerous cases, however, where severe side effects have occurred, raising questions about the efficacy of some treatment. In these cases, the medication upsets the patient's internal balance, causing an unexpected reaction.

Some believe that by maintaining a fully balanced diet, disease and discomfort can be all but eliminated. Followers of this way of thinking report better health, although even this can be taken to extremes that cause imbalance in other areas of life.

Everywhere, there are opposites; day and night, good and bad, love and hate, pain and pleasure, male and female, happiness and sadness, war and peace.

Eastern philosophies attribute much importance to balance and opposites. Two aspects are important. The fact that opposites exist and are necessary to appreciate each is one; the importance and desirability of achieving a balance in life, is the other. Avoidance of excesses in any area is another way of achieving equilibrium—Moderation. Excess in one area is a clear sign of deficiency in another.

Buddhists believe that desire leads to suffering. Anyone who has deeply desired anything (love perhaps, or wealth, or fame) knows that unchecked desire ultimately leads to excess. Buddhists strive for dispassion to extinguish the need for attachments.

Christians are taught to give materially and spiritually to achieve glory. This is essentially also a release of attachment, a calming of excess and desire through balancing what we take in with what we give out—Sharing.

Achieving complete balance in all areas of life is really impossible for humans. However it is a worthwhile goal for which to aim. We all have areas of life that lack balance. Perhaps we hoard things when we should let go, or devote too much time and effort to our job, sport, or hobby. Whatever your area of excess, you know what it is. If you do not know, you will discover it by thinking about it. Knowing what is out of balance enables the smoothing of wrinkles.

The closer we get to this state of equilibrium, the better we are able to handle the upsetting disruptions in life. They will never disappear, problems will always be with us, but with balance, we become better at dealing with them.

With balance we are better able to appreciate and enjoy the good parts too. Balance certainly does not equate to boredom, it equates to a fuller, more satisfied and happier life.

· 12 ·

Everything Has Consequences

There is a universal law of "give and take." Everything in the universe is subject to this law, including humans. This is not a great revelation, but it is a reality that is not acknowledged with sufficient importance by many.

We will look at this from three different vantage points. There are the scientific laws observed in physics, spiritual or religious rules, and the effects we experience directly as our daily lives unfold.

〜

Scientifically, in nature this law is in evidence everywhere around us.

Sir Isaac Newton's third law of motion describes that: "For every action there is an equal and opposite reaction." One thing happens, which causes something else of the same magnitude to occur in the opposite direction.

Numerous cycles operate in nature: day and night, the seasons, moon phases, the tide, birth to death and the list goes on. Scientists are now discovering that even those things we thought were random, like how birds flock and the formation of clouds, fit into patterns or cycles.*

---

* For more on this fascinating field, see the essays Chaos, Miracles And Magic, and Chaos, Karma & Spirituality in Part Four.

These cycles and seemingly chaotic natural phenomena all follow precise rules that essentially follow the cause and effect principle.

In the future, physicists and mathematicians are likely to discover more frequently that nature's laws are a lot less complicated than we expected.

~

From a philosophical, spiritual, or religious perspective, this law is distributed in various forms through just about every philosophy and religion. An eye for and eye; give, and it will be given to you; karma; cause and effect; reward and retribution; and you reap what you sow. These are phrases or words that are commonly used to describe this concept.

Although it is a word used mainly in Hindu and Buddhist teachings, the Sanskrit word *karma* has become more or less universally used to encapsulate the concept of cause and effect into one word, so for simplicity we will use it here as a general-purpose, non-denominational term.

This block of our foundation is important because it provides an explanation for a lot of the things we find contradictory in observing modern life.

The Old Testament's* "eye for eye, tooth for tooth" has the negative tone of punishment for misdeeds—and despite the belief of some that it refers to karma, this verse actually *does* refer to punishment for crimes. By contrast, the New Testament's† "give, and it will be given to you" puts a more positive spin on the law of karma.

The Eastern interpretation of karma does not attach any good or bad connotation. Karma is neither good nor bad. Blame, good,

---

*   Leviticus 24:20

†   Luke 6:38

and bad are merely human (mainly Western) values we apply based on our beliefs.

An analogy: You put your hand in a fire. You get burnt. It is neither punishment nor retribution, good or bad. It is merely a consequence of your action—nothing more, nothing less.

Karma operates in much the same way. Whatever you do, will come back to you in equal measure. It does not mean that if I hit you, you will hit me—although you might! In simplistic terms, we all have a *balance of deeds* that must be worked off. If the balance is "good," we will receive "good" of some kind to the same measure. If the balance is "bad," we will experience "bad" in the same way.

Those who believe in reincarnation find it easier to accept the concept of karma because the operating time scale is so much greater, although it is just as valid without that belief. It is not the purpose of this book to offer persuasion either way on the subject of reincarnation. It is mentioned here because the application of karma is viewed differently (but ultimately with the same consequence) depending upon your belief.

Those of us with a Christian upbringing were usually taught that reincarnation is a fallacy, although the early Church apparently included reincarnation in its doctrine (it was excised in 553 AD at the Council of Constantinople).

The application of karma following the standard Christian teaching of today would occur during this earthly life and/or at Final Judgment.

For those who believe in reincarnation and the ultimate re-unification with the divine, whatever that is perceived to be, the application of karma would occur over a long period of time, encompassing many lives.

In both of these interpretations, the time scale of each karmic event will be spread over too long a period for us to be able to identify or attribute "debits and credits" to specific causes. In any event, just as bank account deposits and withdrawals do not always match each other; karmic transactions are not likely to match each other exactly.

It is not possible to get into explanations regarding other belief systems, as there are countless possibilities. Most readers will have some idea about karma (whatever you wish to call it) and will have their personal views on the subject.

Through my thought process, as mentioned earlier, everything had to make some kind of sense. I find the adoption of karma, as part of the foundation, helps to satisfy many questions to which I have not yet found any other acceptable answer. Questions like: why bad things happen to good people; why children are born with deformities; and why people who cheat, lie and rob seem to thrive, to name just three examples.

~

Looking at day-to-day consequences, we ignore any spiritual or scientific implications, focusing only on the world of human and material interaction. Every time we do or say anything, there are consequences. There are even consequences of *not* doing or saying anything.

We learn this early in life although it is not usually expressed in quite this way. Most of the time, the consequence of our action is exactly what we desire it to be.

We can call the two phases *cause* and *effect*: By picking up a telephone and depressing the buttons in a particular pattern (cause), the telephone makes the necessary connections to make a friend's phone ring (effect). The ring alerts the friend that there is a call (cause), prompting her to pick up the receiver (effect). Picking up the receiver connects the call (cause), allowing the friends to begin a conversation (effect).

Our days are full of these sometimes overlapping and sequential cause and effect cycles. This is as it should be, we do not even think about them most of the time. These small decisions take place subconsciously with the objective of creating an effect.

Then there are times when we react to something or someone without a specific objective in mind. Or we *do* have a specific objective in mind, but without having sufficiently considered the consequences that will actually flow from our actions we cause a different effect or result.

To illustrate: You are busy doing some intricate task that requires concentration. Your young daughter (or son, or sister, brother, niece, neighbor…pick the appropriate relationship) is "helping" you. Continually asking why this, and why that. The distraction causes you to lose concentration. You become frustrated. Just as you nearly have it done…another inane question…you get angry with this child. You just want the questions to stop.

You explode: "Will you just shut-up. Stop asking all those stupid questions!"

That will do it every time. The child stops dead. Now you will definitely not hear any more questions. But the child is hurt beyond words.

You achieved your objective. Depending on your relationship with the child, she may be emotionally scarred for life, even if it is a small scar. You did not really mean to hurt her, so you apologize and try to explain why you said what you did. Hopefully the relationship is mended, but the damage has been done. And what has been done cannot be undone. You did not weigh the consequences before opening your mouth.

We all do things we later regret, but by being more aware of the fact that consequences flow from all actions, we can be more circumspect about what we do and say; framing our actions to achieve the desired consequence.

∼

If we refuse to accept that there is a finite dividing line between each area of our lives or anything in nature, it is not a huge leap to accept karma, or cause and effect, as a natural extension of that nature we know, understand, and from which we are constantly learning more.

· 13 ·

EACH PART OF EACH LIFE
IS IMPORTANT

Life is full of trials and tribulations. Accept it. There is no get-ting around it. It does not matter what kind of life you lead. It makes no difference how much money you have, or where you live. You *will* have troubles. Even so, your life will be easier than some, and worse than others.

Our upbringing has programmed us to believe that good things will happen to good people and bad things will happen to bad people. This does not always appear to be the case, but "good" people will appreciate the good things more and suffer the bad things less.

The true measure of anyone is revealed by how they react to both adversity and good fortune. History is full of stories about people who have overcome extreme hardship. These people have displayed their worth because they faced disaster, persevered anyway, and won.

If there are greater heroes than these, they are those who rise to a level above anything that could be expected, selflessly plac-ing somebody else's wellbeing above their own: the ordinary guy who risked his life to provide shelter to a thousand Tutsi refu-gees during the Rwandan genocide in 1994; the nurses of Gulu, Uganda who ministered to Ebola victims in 2000, fully knowing they were putting their lives at risk (twelve were actually infected by the virus and died).

There are heroes everywhere. Some become well known and famous, but the vast majority does not receive any attention or thanks outside of their little circle of influence. Heroes never do what they do for the fanfare. It is because of who and what they *are*. Some indefinable altruistic quality we cannot help but admire.

All these heroes have faced adversity, and risen to the occasion. Their response to this adversity turned into a positive experience for them and for those around them. This time could be the most important in their lives. If they had chosen the route that (perhaps) most people would have taken, they would not have grown as much.

We all face similar opportunities at some point, where we could stand up and make a difference, or take the easy route. For most, the chance will seldom be as dramatic or as dangerous as for the few mentioned earlier, but you recognize them and make a choice. Personally, I had the opportunity to make a public stand against apartheid and sadly chose not to do so. There are always reasons for our choices, and only time reveals the wisdom (or the folly) of that choice.

The more common, but less sensational problems we face from time to time (like a relationship upheaval or losing a job), present similar choices of reaction: Find the most positive response, or allow resistance to drag us into negativity?

Just as we can take a chance and rise in the face of adversity, we have a choice when enjoying good fortune too. Sharing good fortune adds immeasurably to the joy. Fortune smiles on us partly to see what we will do with it. It is easy to grab the money, love, or whatever the good fortune may be, and hold onto it tightly, in an attempt to bathe in its glory to the exclusion of all others.

Those who know will tell you that you cannot successfully hold tightly onto these things. They have to be shared to prosper. Love is more about giving than receiving and a miser's wealth sours the soul. Shared joy feels best and lasts longest.

Your response to each thing that happens in your life determines whether you grow and flourish, or decline and flounder.

Whether perceived as good or bad, each thing that happens in our lives is important, necessary, and provides lessons for us. We choose whether to learn from each experience or not. We further choose whether it will have a positive or negative effect on the rest of our lives.

By accepting everything as an opportunity to learn, a chance to excel, we make each moment of life even more important and meaningful.

If we cannot be trusted
in what we say and do,
what value can we be.

To anyone or anything?

· 14 ·

INTEGRITY AND HONESTY
ARE INVIOLABLE

Honesty and integrity as desired qualities have become deval-
ued over time. In recent years, heroes and leaders in sport,
politics, religion, and business, have adopted the attitude that the
end justifies the means. They rated their success or short-term
survival higher than moral principles. Many times, this self-serv-
ing position was publicly defended as being in the best interests of
the country, team, company, or some illusory cause—as though
dishonesty is an admirable quality.

Honesty and truthfulness are similar qualities, although
honesty seems to imply an integrity that truth does not.

If I have big ears, I have big ears and that is the truth, but over
time we learn that in many cases, what is true for one person, is
not necessarily true for another.

In most cases, truth depends upon the assumptions, beliefs,
or deductions, which are made prior to arriving at that truth. For
example, Christians believe the Bible is the Word of God. This
provides sufficient validity to accept the contents of the Book as
truth. They find strength and comfort from reading and quoting passages from the Bible. Quoting verses from the Bible to
an atheist, however, is pointless because she does not accept the
premise that the source is infallible.

There is the saying that the truth always hurts. It doesn't always hurt, but it often can. Verbalizing facts with no concern for the effect they will have on others is careless. It does no good to tell a truth where the only result is hurt, fear, distrust, hate, or any other negative effect.

Sometimes the truth will hurt, yet still will have to be told for a particular reason: for example, notifying someone that a loved one has died is obviously necessary.

The essence of honesty, as we use it here, is that we should avoid lying—especially where the lie would get us out of a tight spot. When faced with the need to say something, what is said, must be the truth as we know it. A "white lie" is still a lie. It is better not to speak than to speak an untruth. A life built on dishonesty is a counterfeit existence and each dishonest act reinforces the deception.

We should not only expect honesty of ourselves; we should demand it of those around us too—particularly those in positions of authority who influence situations that directly affect us.

Honesty is a fundamental part of integrity, which refers to living by an ethical or moral code. Together with other principles being laid out in this part of the book, honesty is an essential component.

People do not trust others who they believe are dishonest, and just like trust, integrity has to be earned.

· 15 ·

OUR LIVES ARE OUR OWN
RESPONSIBILITY

Each life consists of the sum of all experiences.
Who and where you are today, is a direct result of everything
that has happened to you since your birth—reincarnation advo-
cates would say even prior to that. Many of these occurrences are
of your own doing; some are because of other people's actions
and decisions—your parents, teachers, and anyone else who has
influenced your life.

Some of us have lived happy, contented, and privileged lives.
Others have had to fight each day to survive. On average, we
have lived a combination of the two. Whatever the case, what
has happened has happened, and there is nothing that will undo
it or change it. We should accept that we are the product of our
past, but that past is now history. It need not negatively impact
on our future.

Although we cannot change the past, we can reinterpret it to
brighten our present and future.

Pop culture thrives upon stories of a pained, troubled past.
These trials and tribulations are frequently offered as an excuse or
justification of excesses in adulthood. Famous people wear their
pain as a badge. Sometimes it seems that Hollywood scripts have
a requirement for the hero to have a tortured past, with periodic
flashbacks, to hinder their progress.

The reality is: we *all* have these experiences, which have negatively affected our development, usually dating from our early years. Hypnosis has been used effectively in both discovering these events, which we often do not consciously remember, and neutralizing the negative effect they exert on present day life.

Interestingly, these experiences generally occur at a pretty young age, some even whilst still in mother's womb. Because the baby or child is still immature, with limited vocabulary or experience to grasp nuances of speech and action, these painful memories can often be a result of a misunderstanding that would not have affected her if she had been a little older and more mature!

Often we are not aware that these situations from our youth are having an effect on our daily lives, but we *are* aware of other more recent events, which affect us. It is fairly common to hold onto negative feelings like hurt, resentment, and anger, whether we can identify the source or not.

Just as people use abusive childhood experiences to justify the way they turned out, it is tempting to use more recent sleights to justify actions that we would not be able to defend any other way.

The way in which a psychologist or hypnotherapist would help someone overcome either a traumatic past or a negative emotion that is limiting her ability to reach her goal is to analyze the event, and then offer a different perspective; to put a different light on it. There is *always* something positive to be learnt from any experience.

By reinterpreting the process, instead of having a negative, destructive effect, there can be a positive, constructive outcome.

As an individual, it may not be possible to achieve the same results for deeply buried pain, but knowing about the process can help to understand why we do what we do. We can also look at current emotional slings and arrows and dodge the effect they would otherwise have.

Rather than allow the past (particularly the pain) to dictate your present and future, you have the ability to take charge of your life from this very moment. You do this by accepting responsibility for all that happens to you and for all that you do.

Some things are outside your control, and you need to adapt to these, but if you shirk responsibility for yourself and for your actions, how can you expect anyone else to accept responsibility? Even though there are circumstances you cannot control, you *can* control your response to those circumstances.

It is easy to blame others for our misfortunes; however justified it may seem at the time. This is a trap from which it is difficult to escape. It becomes a habit. Anyone who tried to give up smoking will tell you how difficult it is to break a habit. And a habit that lets you off the hook is even more obstinate.

There was a phrase in real estate circles that goes something like this: "If you want to be more successful, buy a new car."

The reasoning behind this being if you put yourself in debt and commit to covering the debt, you will be motivated to do what it takes to achieve additional sales. It may seem ridiculous, but the fact is, our performance in all areas of life is heavily influenced by our state of mind.

The purpose of advertising is to influence people to buy a particular product. This is achieved by motivating the consumer to desire the advertised product. Motivation is a state of mind.

By accepting responsibility for everything in our lives, we remove the inclination to pass blame for our misfortune onto other people or circumstances. With this approach, the focus shifts from a feeling of hopelessness to one of possibility. Now when faced with a setback, instead of complaining about forces outside our control, we turn to assessing the situation and devising a solution, either to turn the setback into a windfall, or minimize the negative effect and provide a valuable lesson.

This is a really significant shift in consciousness. It can completely overhaul lives. Like most changes we choose to make, a small beginning quickly expands and becomes a normal part of life.

This is an involved concept that is closely linked to other areas, which we will address as well, especially the choices we make (in the next chapter), the effect of positivity, and forgiveness—so this is not the final word.

For this principle, the bottom line is that there are ways to let go of the pain from the past so that it will no longer pull you back. In Part Three, which deals with practical steps, we will take a closer look at this.

∾

Being attracted to gadgets and electronic gizmos, I am often offered "peace of mind" in the form of extended warranties on things I buy.

The sales person is often amused when I tell her that I don't need one: "...because things I buy don't break down."

The look I receive tells me she thinks I'm joking, but it is not a joke. Things I buy really do not give trouble. I expect them to give faithful service, and invariably they do.

Similarly, in parking lots we seldom have trouble finding a convenient spot—in my case this would be a bay where someone is not likely to bash my car as they open their doors.

I expect to find these convenient places, and they are usually waiting there when I arrive.

These are two fun examples of how taking responsibility for our lives can provide positive power!

· 16 ·

Life Consists Of Our Choices

Everything you do, and everything you don't do, results from a conscious or unconscious decision that was made based upon your priorities at the time. When we take responsibility for our lives, we also take responsibility for the choices we make—often without even knowing we are really making a choice.

At any given moment unless we are sleeping (and maybe even then) we are evaluating numerous options, whether to do this or not: whether to do that or not.

Should I continue what I am doing, or take a break? Should I scratch that itch on my cheek now, or wait and see whether it disappears? I am thirsty; maybe I should get a drink of water now. Perhaps I should call so-and-so now to arrange a meeting. Let me check my e-mail quickly before continuing. And so on...

Any number of reasons may be given for not doing something we had previously agreed to do, or which we now feel guilty for not having done. One of the most common today, is: "I just didn't have time to get to it." Others are: "Something cropped up. I couldn't put it off and just *had* to sort it out," or perhaps with more honesty: "It just slipped my mind."

Because of the culture in large businesses today, it is common for men (and women, although probably less frequently) to get so involved with the current crisis that they "forget" to get home in time for a dinner date, or pick up the children from some after school activity, or whatever. When completely immersed in any task, we tend to allocate our full mental resources to that task, often to the exclusion of all other considerations.

This is an effective method of coping with crises, of problem solving. In times of crisis it is sometimes important to filter out extraneous factors. We are not suggesting that the blocking of unrelated, unconnected considerations is necessarily a bad thing. It certainly has a place, but it is useful to understand the process and realize when it is used. And when it impacts adversely on other parts of our lives, we acknowledge the reason; perhaps learning to control it effectively.

Nowadays, there are far more demands for our time and attention than our forebears would have imagined possible. We could say that it is understandable to overlook something we planned, or undertook to do, however it is unlikely that you would forget your wedding, or the date you leave on vacation, or any other important occasion in your life.

The reason we remember these crucial dates, and times, is simply that we make a point of remembering them. Perhaps we note the time in our diary, or put a note on the refrigerator.

When we forget something, it is because we consciously or unconsciously allow something else to become more important to us. It really is that simple.

Even when we feel forced into a situation and believe we have no choice, this is not true. We *always* have a choice. The options available may not be those we would prefer, but there are options. To accept or decline, acquiesce or protest, fight or run, stay or go.

At times, the only acceptable choice is so obvious that it seems there is no alternative, but a choice is still made—even if the choice is to *not* make a choice and allow matters to unfold.

It all boils down to choices. What matters most at this moment takes priority. To take complete responsibility for our lives requires taking responsibility for all our choices, even those we prefer to disown.

· 17 ·

PUMP UP THE POSITIVE.
NEUTRALIZE THE NEGATIVE

This is very important to happiness and emotional wellbeing. It is worth spending considerable time and effort on this one area alone.

Our self-esteem reflects the extent that we believe ourselves to be worthy of respect. Another way of defining this would be that our level of self-esteem is equal to the balance of all the positive and negative experiences of our lives.

We all have a shortage of self-esteem. None of us really believe ourselves to be worthy enough. The extent of our true worth is way beyond anything we imagine. The reason for this is that we all absorb far more negative influence than positive.

From the moment we are born, we begin absorbing influences and experiences, which are then stored in our memory. Actually, hypnotherapy case studies indicate this may begin before birth, but it is not important here to pin down the exact moment when memory is activated.

There is more understanding of the effect of positive and negative conditioning now than there was in previous times. It seems that children growing up today will reach adulthood with greater feelings of self worth than generations who grew during those years when parents were less aware of the extent that parenting affects children's self esteem.

During the fifties, sixties and earlier, for example, strict discipline was enforced on most children, often with beatings for reinforcement. It was very much a philosophy of: "Spare the rod and spoil the child."

It is not that the parents of those times were delinquent in their parenting or that they loved their offspring less; for the most part, they did the best they knew how. They just did not know as much as we do today.

Then again, children in those times had far less exposure to many of the negative influences and pressures with which today's children have to contend.

In our early years, the people we look up to affect us enormously: parents, teachers, clergy, aunts, uncles, older siblings, and so on. During this time, we are negatively affected by experiences that would not have the same effect on an adult. An example of this may be the cause for a child to become afraid of the dark. Often misunderstandings result in a negative charge being registered in the mind: for example overhearing parents loudly arguing at night and fearing that a divorce will follow can associate darkness with fear.

As we grow, we become more influenced by the world around us. Television, video games, advertising, sporting heroes, and school friends are a few. Eventually we enter the workforce, absorbing all the new influences there too.

Even ignoring all the uncontrolled influences on the young, looking at how our world operates today, there is little wonder that we build up a "positivity imbalance".

At school, in sport and at work, we are exhorted to do better, achieve more, and work harder; implying that we are deficient. Add to this every time we are rejected in any way: having a bank loan application turned down; being dumped by a boyfriend, girlfriend, or spouse; or even entering a competition we do not win.

At various times you may have been told that you are too tall, or short, thin, fat, dark, light, old, young, pretty or plain.

Perhaps you succumbed to peer pressure when a teenager and started smoking. Later realizing the error of your ways, you attempt to stop. Because you believed the stories you've heard, you thought you were addicted to smoking, so your attempt to quit failed; possibly followed by many more attempts over the years. Each failure reinforces your belief that you are addicted and cannot give it up. At the same time this compounds the feeling of inferiority. After all, lots of other people are able to give up!

Or perhaps it was fighting a weight problem. With essentially the same result from successive failed bouts of dieting. Trying each new program that becomes popular, none of them work for you. You ask yourself: "What is wrong with me?"

Advertising works to create desire for each product being sold. To do this, advertisers subtly tell us we are not worthy because we do not drive the right car, or use the best cosmetics, or live in the right neighborhood. They imply that the only way to become worthy is to buy whatever they are selling. If we bought their wares, we would feel complete and all desire would evaporate. We would become one of the "beautiful people."

Of course the reality seldom lives up to the promise, so we feel even more unworthy. We are bombarded with these messages everywhere, each one compounding that "not quite good enough" and "if only" message.

Both movies and magazines parade all the beautiful, rich, perfectly built and complexioned people whose lives are (apparently) perfect before us.

Adding more to this cauldron, government sometimes seems to favor a fearful populace. At every turn they warn of a monster out to get you. It may be an opposing political party or a threatening ideology, a terrorist, or someone who is just *too* different. These messages reinforce insecurity, a position favored for mass manipulation and propaganda.

As if all these influences are not enough to pull us right down, most of us were taught to be humble about our achievements; to play down those things that make us feel proud, powerful, or just plain good. Boasting about our victories is considered unbecoming.

And on top of all this, or perhaps because if it, we often pick up the destructive habit of making disparaging remarks about ourselves and our abilities.

Offsetting all these negative jolts, are the positive things we have experienced throughout our lives. That time when you won a prize, graduated, or when someone important to you told you how good you looked. When you got a promotion at work, or noticed that look of love in your child's eyes, the pride you felt for creating that perfect little human being.

Thousands of these wonderful, positive times occur during an average lifetime, but there are never enough to outweigh the negatives. We live in an adversarial society, and where there is confrontation, there will always be a loser. We see it in life; there are always fewer winners than contestants. And even winners do not win at everything, although we will often not notice their failings.

Happily, this is not the whole story. This list of potentially damaging influences and the typically out-of-balance effect they produce is reversible. There are a number of simple, practical steps you can take to improve this "positivity imbalance".

These are covered in detail in Part Three. You can cultivate a constant awareness of the effect your surroundings have on your positivity balance. This will allow you to fulfill the promise of your talents and abilities much better.

· 18 ·

<u>Sometimes, What Is, Is</u>

W e all want to lead better lives. We want more than we cur-
rently have for both our families and ourselves. This drive
to improve our lot is the force behind most of the inventions and
innovations developed through history. It has provided the impetus for all of the conveniences we take for granted today and
without which we would have trouble living.

Obviously this is a vital and helpful attribute for humankind
to possess, but there is also a less desirable side to it.

When we are dissatisfied with a situation or circumstance,
we often resist it. Where this resistance motivates action that results in a satisfactory result, this is good. We change something
for the better; generating a feeling of achievement, beating the
odds and overcoming difficulties. Other times though, the situation is one we cannot change. For example, as a private individual, we cannot usually change government policy. We cannot
stop the wind blowing. We cannot make everyone hold the same
opinions we do. There is an endless list of things we cannot directly influence.

Some people waste a tremendous amount of energy over
things, circumstances, events, or people that displease them. By
allowing ourselves to be diverted, resisting those things we cannot change, we squander energy that would be better spent on
those things we *can* affect.

If something exists, it exists whether we wish to acknowledge it or not. Fighting or resisting facts, serve no constructive purpose. Each time we do, we add to any feelings of incompetence, and add another negative to the balance in our mind.

Accepting that a situation exists certainly should not be interpreted as meekly accepting or condoning a distasteful circumstance just because we don't have the personal means to change it.

It is commonly accepted that for alcoholics to overcome their problem, they must first acknowledge that the problem exists, that they are in fact alcoholics. In the same way, solving a problem is virtually impossible without first noticing that there is a problem. So, accepting the *existence* of conditions we don't like, stimulates the process of devising a plan to overcome the problem.

We need to be reasonable in our expectations though. It is unlikely that we would be able to get a committee together to work towards stopping the wind blowing, but we could certainly mobilize people to lobby the government to change an unacceptable policy.

Some would say there are no limits to what can be achieved, even including the blowing of the wind, and this may be true; however the point here, is that there are some things we just have to accept as being the way they are—either because we cannot change them immediately; we cannot change them in the available time; or the effort to make the change is not worthwhile either in time, money or effort.

It is best to let these things go. Don't waste time allowing them to frustrate you. Your energy is better spent on something more constructive. Remember, accepting reality does not mean condoning it.

Compartmentalizing the mind is a process that is easier for some than for others, but, as with most mental techniques, practice enhances the ability. Moving your mental focus from the problem and focusing on some other absorbing task or thought, is the easiest way. What this does is move the troubling idea into the background, allowing you to carry on with life. At the same time, the mind's natural problem solving mechanism starts working on possible solutions.

Often this will result in an idea: a way to change things, or maybe a different perspective that diminishes the "hassle factor" of the situation. Other times there is no solution forthcoming. We learn to live with the problem for the time being, recognizing that it exists, whilst also recognizing that we have no influence over it for the present.

Part Three includes techniques to develop this acceptance of what is.

The Moving Finger writes; and, having writ,
Moves on: nor all thy Piety nor Wit
    Shall lure it back to cancel half a Line,
Nor all thy Tears wash out a Word of it.

~ The Rubáiyát of Omar Khayyám: L1
translated by Edward Fitzgerald, 1859

· 19 ·

WHAT IS DONE IS DONE

These five words describe a truth that, if universally recognized, would revolutionize the world!

A few of the building blocks already discussed touch on elements of this one. We can view this from two perspectives: in terms of the past and its effect on us, and in terms of possible futures.

One of the fundamental principles behind the success of a huge number of cases treated by psychiatrists, psychologists, hypnotherapists, and others; is that unresolved remorse, guilt and negative emotion, can be cruelly crippling.

The doctrine of confession and forgiveness practiced by the Christian Church (whether formally or informally) has been responsible for thousands of conversions to Christianity. What this confession essentially does is allow the confessor to let go of destructive feelings and emotions that have a source in the past, by handing them over to God. This leads to a feeling of elation and release, of a weight having been lifted*.

It is a sad truth that all of us have skeletons in our past. There is some conflicted hurt holding us back from our authentic potential. Letting go of the hurtful past, how ever this is achieved, opens up a brand new, lighter vision of the world around us.

Compartmentalization of the mind, as described in the previous chapter, is not appropriate here because in a sense, this

---

* See also Chapter 44: "The Healing Mind".

is what caused this problem in the first place; repressing emotional pain.

Healing these emotional scars that come back to haunt us—often in ways we would never recognize—is best done by using the process of forgiveness. Sometimes the person to be forgiven is someone else, often a parent or teacher; sometimes it is the tormented person herself.

There are several ways to arrive at this state of release. Besides the two already mentioned (therapy and religion), there are probably dozens more that get to the same result using different methodologies. Some kind of penance may be necessary, while others give almost immediate relief. All tend to require a conscious, subconscious, or symbolic connection to the source event or emotion.

Successful and complete forgiveness (there may be several episodes requiring forgiveness) releases the claws of the past. This process is widely supported by case studies.

Now looking to the future, realizing how easily people are thrown off balance, often without this being the intention, we guard against allowing those claws to sharpen and start pulling us back into past patterns.

Keeping those claws trimmed is most effective by being vigilant. We now know how the claws grew in the first place. Situations that give rise to those familiar feelings of dread have to be dealt with or avoided immediately. For example, if someone says or does something that gives rise to those feelings, it is often sufficient to recognize the cause and let the person know politely that you do not like (or feel comfortable with) whatever is causing your distress. If for some reason you cannot handle the situation, it may be best to remove yourself from it.

These are very broad and simple examples. Each person and condition is different. What is appropriate in one circumstance may not be so in another, consequently, an entirely different response may be more fitting.

~

Realizing that we are all interconnected, that all things have consequences, and how delicate the balance between freedom and mental bondage is, we should also take more care over the effect we have on others.

In personal interaction, once we have done or said something, it is impossible to reverse the hurt. A harsh word remains a harsh word, whether we regret it or not. A destructive action remains destructive even if we apologize. The harm cannot be undone. At best it can only be mitigated. Even then, mitigation is really more useful for the offender, because it reduces guilt; it does not do much to help the offended, particularly when she is a sensitive soul.

To illustrate, look at the example of a man telling his wife that he has been unfaithful to her. He may be remorseful. He apologizes. He feels better for the confession. Does the wife feel the same way about their relationship as she did before her husband's revelation? No. She may try to forgive him, but the damage is done. It cannot be repaired once the cat is out of the bag. The relationship may survive, but this episode will not be forgotten.

One effective way to guard against causing pain to others is to embed this question in your mind: "What do I want the end result of this to be?"

Repeating behavior is how habits are formed, and this is exactly what will happen with this question. By asking yourself this each time a tricky situation arises, you stop yourself from unconsidered actions and responses.

In the example of the unfaithful husband, it would have been best for him to honor his commitment to be faithful to his wife. If he failed in that, given the fact that he transgressed, there could be no good result from admitting his indiscretion to his wife.

His best course of action would be to ask himself the question: "How do I want this to turn out?"

He must decide whether he wants to recommit to his marriage. If he does, then the adultery should be stopped immediately and he should work on whatever feeling was behind the misconduct. All relationships take work.

If, on the other hand, he no longer wishes to (or is unable to) remain faithfully in the marriage, he must end it to be fair to his wife even though this will still produce pain.

This is an example based on an imaginary situation. It is not suggested as the final word on morality or marriage. In real life things are not always clear-cut and there could well be other perfectly acceptable solutions depending on actual circumstances and the personalities involved.

∾

Whether you accept it or not, the past has already occurred. There is nothing you can do to change it. Just as we need to accept that there are things we cannot control as discussed in the previous chapter, we are best served by accepting that the past—all the way from birth to this very moment; whatever it contains—is not reversible. History cannot be undone.

We are then able to take steps to prevent or minimize the effect it exerts on our life (and other lives too) from here onward.

· 20 ·

OFTEN, ANY DECISION IS
BETTER THAN NONE

Numerous major decisions have to be made during the course of a lifetime. Deciding whether to marry a particular person, which car or house to buy, and whether to accept a job offer or not, are a few of the larger and more common choices. These big questions have to be carefully considered before arriving at an answer.

There are an infinite number of other decisions that have to be made where it is not possible to determine exactly which conclusion is the most suitable. This is also sometimes the case with major decisions. It may be that there is a subjective element to the decision, or perhaps some facts that could influence a decision are not available or apparent. Sometimes the decision boils down to a simple choice that really has no right or wrong. A lot of the time, which way the decision goes has little or no lasting effect on anything—it is really little more than a momentary preference; a whim.

Most of the time, we intuitively know what the correct decision is to any question, but we resist making that choice for one reason or another. It may be through fear of making mistakes, or simply resisting the choice that we know is best. It is possible for anyone to develop this intuition; it merely takes practice and trust in the process.

There are innumerable "systems" being used for reaching decisions. Some people use simple external processes such as tossing a coin, employing a dowsing tool, and divining cards amongst others. For many though, these methods seem too arbitrary or esoteric.

A generally recommended method of arriving at the best decision is to split a sheet of paper into two columns, then list all the pros in one and all the cons in the other. Sometimes a (subjective) value is allocated to each point, then each column is totaled. Whichever column has the highest score is the best solution. . This is intended to help come to a rational decision untainted by subjective or emotional considerations.

This approach is useful at times, but not always so. One purpose it does serve well however, is gathering facts and considerations that are applicable to the question. Another worthwhile step, particularly for important decisions, is to ask the opinion of others—but the purpose of this should not be so they can make the decision for you. These other opinions can be especially useful in adding previously unconsidered perspective to the question. Once all the relevant facts and options have been gathered, the choice remains yours.

Procrastination in decision-making can have a debilitating effect, as each evasion embeds the habit and reinforces the belief that we are incapable of deciding.

The only true way to avoid mistakes is to stop making decisions completely. If you stop making mistakes, you stop learning. Mistakes are nature's way of teaching us how to make better choices – they are a gentle implementation of the survival-of-the-fittest process. By trying, we become fitter and better survivors. We have to take some chances and accept that sometimes they will be the wrong ones.

Where there is no way to arrive at exactly the most fitting choice, where there is little difference between the possible results, any decision is better than none.

With all decisions, though, it is important not to second-guess that determination.

Following each decision is a sequence of steps or further choices that have to be made. Once a decision is made, follow it through to its conclusion unless or until some new factor becomes apparent to indicate that a different choice would have been more suitable. If this happens, then assess the cost and implications of changing that decision and come to a revised conclusion if appropriate.

There is an aspect of this point, also related to the previous chapter, which is important to mention. When we realize that we may not have chosen the best option. It is tempting to get into a cycle, which starts out with the thought: "I should have ..."

This frame of mind is like stepping onto quicksand. The "should have ... could have ... would have ..." syndrome builds and reinforces a feeling of inadequacy and hopelessness, further inhibiting our decision-making ability. The choices we made have been made. Whatever action followed each choice has already occurred. We all make mistakes and bad decisions, but what is done, is done.

Once we realize that an alternative choice would have been more appropriate, we can take action either to reverse it or, at least, minimize the detrimental effect of the decision. This is a far more positive and practical response.

The more decisive you become, the better your decisions get. Work on the simple ones, and graduate to the larger ones. Learn from any mistakes.

Just as beauty is in the eye of the beholder,
truth is in the mind of the proponent.

Most of what we hold to be true,
cannot be proven to be true,
and should therefore be treated as
no more than conjecture, opinion or belief.

Regardless of the fervor of that belief,
it is quite possible for something to be
completely true and self evident to you,
yet inconceivable to me.

· 21 ·

PERSONAL OPINIONS AND
BELIEFS ARE SACRED

A war is quietly raging for control of your mind, and there is an immense amount of money and power at stake.

This is not a paranoid conspiracy theorist's rant that is better suited to some science fiction fantasy. Nor is it about people finding ways to implant microchips in our brains.

Everyone has an agenda—some point of view we want to propagate. Advertisers want you to buy their product; politicians want you to vote for them; employers want you to work hard for the smallest paycheck possible; parents want children to behave; schools want children to abide by the rules, and to conform to their norms.

Everywhere we are subjected to somebody's opinions. Media of all kinds is everywhere: mobile phone text messages, the Internet, e-mail, television, radio, newspapers, magazines, billboards—to mention just the main ones, are constantly bombarding us with information, much of it no more than speculation or subjective bias.

The term "subjective bias" refers to the fairly common practice of applying a *slant* to a story or report. We all do it to some extent. Even the way we interpret the world is slanted or biased according to our general attitude, which is based largely on our past (experience, influences, and education). There is the often-used example of the drinking glass containing water up to the half way mark – it is said that optimists see it as half full, while pessimists see it as half empty.

Perhaps the truth is that whether the glass is half full or half empty depends upon how the water got to that level – was it filled to that level (half full), or was it emptied to that level (half empty). Or maybe it is just a glass of water, neither full nor empty.

Lack of complete information skews any conclusion. This can be, and is, used to manipulate opinions and perceptions. It has become a common practice of opinion-molders to quote statistics which support their views. These seem thorough, convincing, and conclusive to most of us.

Statistics are essentially just an interpretation of a collection of answers to specific questions. This in itself invalidates many results unless *all* the relevant questions have been asked. It may seem obvious that this would be the case, but it is not always so. A deception we blindly accept. After all, numbers don't lie do they?

By judiciously selecting the questions to be asked, statistics can be used to back up virtually any opinion. Even where this is not done, where all relevant factors are included; the way statistics are interpreted can tremendously influence the message they deliver.

To illustrate this, an emotive subject that periodically arises in just about every city of the world is that of road accidents and fatalities. Whenever there is an increase in either of these, citizens and public officials call for a reduction in speed limits.

Conventional wisdom says "speed kills"—in some countries you can even see signs proclaiming this on the roadside. This belief arises from the statistical fact that most road deaths and serious injuries, over a period of time, occur on the streets that permit higher speeds. Often, at least one of the vehicles involved was traveling fast.

Looking only at the speed question, it is easy to conclude that speed is the culprit. It is verifiable from witness reports. However if speed were causing these accidents, there would be far more serious pile-ups at motor races, considering that they reach speeds far higher than any legal limit. From this comparison alone we can deduce that there are obviously other factors that heavily influence the occurrence of accidents.

It seems more likely that the main cause of accidents is bad driving. *Inappropriate* speed is undoubtedly a factor, but so are drugs, alcohol, tiredness, road-worthiness, weather conditions, cell-phones, and spilling coffee.

It is easier and more profitable to control speed, since it is often a factor, so this is where the emphasis for most traffic enforcement agencies is placed.

The point of the past few paragraphs is to illustrate that without questioning and considering things, it is easy to be misled into believing something which is not necessarily the whole story.

For many, the pace of modern life allows little time for contemplation. Even those times when we are not actively involved in earning a living or attending to the other demands of life, we are often preoccupied with thoughts of those things. This leaves little time to think actively about anything that is not urgently demanding attention.

Everybody knows it is prudent to monitor our food intake. It is potentially *more* important to attend to what gets into our minds. History indicates that the spread of unacceptable beliefs or behavior like racism and other forms of discrimination could be blamed in part on the unquestioned acceptance of extreme views by the masses—think of Hitler's treatment of Jews and South Africa's apartheid policies[*].

These were instances of excessive use of the power of indoctrination, but propaganda is not dead. It is alive and well and being used every day. The trouble is that nowadays it is more

---

[*] For a personal look back at growing up in apartheid South Africa, see Chapter 42: "The Closing Of The Minds".

insidious. Sometimes the intent is to mislead, but its purpose is always to influence others.

In an earlier section, it was suggested that a good way to avoid unintentionally getting yourself into trouble is to ask the question, "What do I want the end result of this to be?"

When you are on the receiving end, a good way to avoid getting your mind into trouble is to ask the question: "What do *they* want the end result to be, and *why*?" Many times, the answer to this question will be acceptable to you. The purpose of this questioning is not to become paranoid about everyone's motives; but to help you safeguard your integrity and to allow you to make informed choices and decisions based on your own values.

Your beliefs and opinions are for you to safeguard. If it becomes apparent to you that these opinions and beliefs no longer fit you, you should change them in the light of new information, once you have evaluated it.

You really cannot believe everything you read, see, or hear. Radio and television stations have twenty-four hours to fill; newspapers have to draw readers to attract advertisers, as do magazines. Sometimes, objectivity suffers. Add to this the ease with which technology permits manipulation of sound, images, and video.

Always be asking "Why?" Be aware; make your own choices and decisions. It is your mind, use it, or lose it.

· 22 ·

ALL FEELINGS ARE GOOD

Every feeling has a purpose: to deliver a message. But when we experience unpleasant feelings, instead of heeding the message, we tend to do things to distract us from the message. Continued distraction of these feelings is destructive. Some of the more common things we use to distract ourselves are smoking, alcohol, food, and drugs; but they also include anything else we do to escape temporarily, any unpleasant feelings we experience such as boredom, anxiety, and fear.

Often these distractions are potentially destructive acts, like self-mutilation—which could range from compulsive scratching or fingernail biting, to slicing body parts. Other times they will seem fairly innocuous, even desirable, like obsessive tidying or cleaning.

The main problem with these distractions is that they only provide brief, limited relief from the unpleasant feeling demanding diversion. They have no meaningful effect on the actual cause of the feeling.

Probably the most common of these destructive distractions are smoking, drinking, and drug abuse (whether legal or not), so we will concentrate on these, although what follows refers just as much to all other diversions like excessive eating, shopping and sex. Even otherwise healthy pursuits like exercise can be used as a distracter and become harmful physically and psychologically.

Calvin Banyan, author of the book "The Secret Language Of Feelings," proclaims that: "All feelings are good," and describes the spiral effect of this process of diverting unpleasant feelings effectively.

It begins with a feeling you do not like: anxiety or grief, perhaps. In an attempt to escape that horrible feeling, you indulge in one of the distractions; let's say alcohol. This provides temporary relief as your senses are dulled. But soon the feeling returns as the effect of drinking wears off and you feel unhappy again, so you indulge again. This begins a cycle requiring ever-greater consumption as you keep returning to that same unhappy feeling, possibly with added guilt for excessive drinking making you feel even worse.

Drinking becomes a habit. Because there is no relief, this habit leads to frustration so you drink even more. And the cycle between distraction and dissatisfaction continues. The frustration then escalates into depression. Unchecked, this spiraling emotional ride will ultimately lead to hopelessness and death by suicide or some other means. The diagram opposite illustrates this spiraling cycle graphically.

This example uses a destructive diversion. A less harmful one could be used instead. In fact, it is possible to find a *constructive* distraction, although that is not usually the way it develops.

Sometimes, realizing there is a problem and understanding the process, one can cultivate a good habit (preferably not illegal, immoral or fattening!) to offset the feeling of unhappiness. Eat carrots instead of chocolate maybe, but only if you enjoy carrots. This kind of distraction will be just as short lived as the destructive kind, but it will not bear the negative effects. It is not the solution.

The only real solution is to deal with the cause of the problem. Understanding the process of these distracting behaviors empowers us to identify the true problem. Instead of treating the symptom, we can now treat the cause.

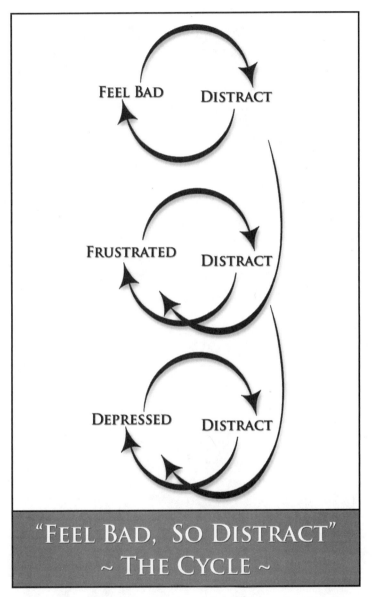

"FEEL BAD, SO DISTRACT"
~ THE CYCLE ~

This graphic is used with permission from Calvin D. Banyan, adapted from his book *The Secret Language of Feelings*, published by Banyan Publishing, Inc.

When next you notice the desire for your particular distraction, stop and ask yourself which feeling is causing you distress. Even a guess at this stage would be okay. Then check on the cause of that feeling. Now you know the purpose for the feeling—it appeared to notify you of the problem.

Once you know the cause of your emotional upset, the solution can be worked on.

Often just knowing the real cause of the problem will relieve the effect it has on you. Other times, it will require more effort. Approaching the person responsible for the upset (that person might be *you*) to work out a solution may be the answer. Or, you may need assistance to arrive at a satisfactory conclusion. Each situation is different.

We get into more depth on this subject; the identification of the cause and the elimination of the effect in Part Three.

· 23 ·

FORGIVENESS IS FOR YOU NOT THE OTHER PERSON

At one time or another, we all seem to hold a grudge against someone for some real or imagined transgression. It is natural for us to feel offended when somebody whom we trust lets us down, lies to us, or "does us wrong". While this hurt is natural and forms part of life's learning process, retaining that hurt, and allowing it to fester, is not.

Open wounds, whether of a physical or psychological nature, serve no worthwhile purpose. Physical wounds are cleaned and cared for to ensure they do not get infected before healing can take place. Psychological (or emotional, if you prefer) wounds should be cared for in much the same way. It takes knowledge and attention to prevent potentially catastrophic emotional infection.

As adults, there are essentially two main reasons (which could work together) for holding onto these destructive emotions. One is to hold the transgression against the perpetrator to use as a weapon—for revenge. The other is to give yourself a reason, really a justification, for your own perceived or real shortcomings.

The sad truth is that the revenge angle seldom, if ever, actually works the way it is intended. Sometimes true reconciliation results from this tactic, but it is not the usual outcome and there are better ways to achieve it. More often, further resentment will be engendered on both sides of the confrontation, which, if allowed to escalate, will end up in a spiraling downward slide for the relationship. Other times, the "perpetrator" will ignore the whole matter: either not recognizing that a problem exists, or refusing any responsibility for it.

Holding onto resentment and wearing it as a badge, blaming this external cause for a personal deficiency, tends to exacerbate the wound and further entrench the shortcoming. We are trained to do things that are justified; we feel that justification gives us permission to do them.

In South Africa during apartheid, it was not possible to buy certain products legally because of the boycotts enforced by governments and some private companies. Products such as computer software, television programming, and music were some of the wares included in these bans. Because these things were not available legally, piracy was rife and some businesses openly traded in (or used) this illegally obtained, boycotted material. People felt justified in enjoying these products the only way they could, and so felt no responsibility for what was effectively stealing.

It was either the South African government or the boycotting company's fault that the otherwise law-abiding citizens were deprived of this stuff!

Similarly, once the blame for anything has been placed elsewhere, we feel justified in disregarding the social or moral constraints that would otherwise have prevented us from behaving in a particular way.

So to elaborate, let us look at a simplified scenario we have used before reflecting a situation that occurs too frequently: A man cheats on his wife. She finds out, and is naturally devastated. Perhaps the marriage breaks down and they separate. There was a time she may have shouldered some of the blame for the break. But he is the dog that did wrong, and she feels cheated, holding her ex-husband totally responsible for the break-up of her family.

Previously just a social drinker, she begins drinking heavily to cope. Due to the escalating drinking, her life starts falling apart. In her mind now, she is not responsible for any of this. The whole thing is his fault, and this is the only way she can face the world. She sees him with his new girlfriend, and resents both of them for being happy. It drives her deeper into the bottle and the cycle carries her towards depression.

This is not a happy lady! The end result of her holding onto the pain and hurt is one she would never have chosen for herself. For her ex-husband, the end result is a good, happy relationship.

Who wins and who loses?

This illustration is admittedly very simple and subjective, but it clearly reflects situations in which people find themselves, even though specific circumstances differ and frequently do not actually take over the person's life. But once on the slippery slope it is very difficult to get back to level, dry ground.

The only really effective way for most people to free themselves from this trap is to find a way of letting go of whatever is behind the negative emotion that holds them captive. A really effective (perhaps the only) method is to forgive the perpetrator.

Forgive and forget. This is a phrase often used to indicate moving-on. While forgiveness is suggested as an effective way to get a life back, let us be clear: the forgiveness we are talking about in this section has absolutely nothing to do with forgetting. If we forget, we lose the benefit of anything we can learn from the experience. We need to remember.

What forgiveness is, and what it is not:

Forgiveness is all about *you*—nobody else. It is something that you do for yourself. It is a process that allows you to release yourself from crippling emotions, leaving all the hurt behind. It sets you free. Forgiveness does not mean that you condone what was done. It does not mean you like the person who hurt you, nor does it mean you forget what they did. Forgiveness will not change the person you forgive.

They will not feel any better about what they did to you. They will not even know you have forgiven them, and there is no need for them ever to know, unless you choose to tell them.

Paradoxically, forgiving ourselves for allowing those bad things to happen to us is often a worthwhile step in reinforcing the changes—even though in reality we may not have had any responsibility for what happened to us.

There are countless methods of forgiveness. It can be achieved through prayer and meditation. So-called "New Age" processes also use forgiveness, although they may be called something else. The "talk therapy" professionals also use forgiveness as a methodology to release negative forces within us. Hypnotherapists usually include forgiveness prominently in their treatments.

How to forgive without going to a shrink? Ultimately, forgiveness consists of recognizing, at an emotional level, that the person who hurt you is also a flawed victim of their own circumstances; realizing that what they did to you was really more about *them*, than it was about you; and then recognizing that you were not responsible for what they did. What they did, was their decision, not yours.

This is an overview of a process. Lasting forgiveness is best accomplished at a deeper level than normal day-to-day consciousness.

· 24 ·

Good Selfishness

We are taught from an early age that thinking of ourselves first, is anti-social. Putting your interests before those of others is just wrong. Throughout our lives, stories of brave, selfless heroes reinforce this teaching.

This had the effect of people, particularly women, sacrificing their dreams and ambitions to help others achieve theirs. One noticeable sign of this is a very common inability of people (once again mainly women) to say "no" because that would be too selfish. After all, the other person's desires are more worthy than our own, aren't they?

Looking into the life-history of people who have really made it in life: artists, musicians, movie stars, business people, philosophers, politicians, or religious leaders, we find that one trait, they all seem to possess, is the drive to succeed; whichever way that success is measured. To achieve their goals, this desire supersedes all others. Virtually every action is aimed at the furtherance of that objective. Some are prepared to sacrifice anything or anyone to reach the pinnacle they desire.

Which of these is right? The woman who cannot say "no" to anything, or the businessman, who is so focused on what he wants that he doesn't consider anyone else? As with so much in life, it is not that simple, but there is a general rule that can be applied in most cases: Excess of anything is not good. Moderation is a good rule to live by in all things. Once we go to extremes, our judgment is skewed and we lose our ability to be objective or rational. It is good to help others; even to go out of our way to help them, but there is a limit to how far we should be prepared to bend to their will.

We should acknowledge our own needs and desires, and so should the people around us. To expect us to abandon our own interests is unreasonable and unfair. We need to create certain boundaries to protect ourselves. Intrusion beyond these boundaries is not welcome. In practice, there will actually be several sets of boundaries; the boundary for a spouse, for example, would differ from that of a work acquaintance.

You could be offended by inappropriate comments or by the actions of someone you don't know. Our society defines the boundaries of social interaction (sometimes through legislation) in these circumstances, but they only go so far.

Everyone is different. You know better than anyone else how comfortable you are with any given situation. You know best what you want out of life. If anyone encroaches into areas you are not comfortable with (for whatever reason), you have a duty to yourself to impose limits. Your boundaries are not barricades, but they *are* a requirement for your self-preservation.

We all enter this world with a reservoir of potential. Some believe the achievement of this potential is our sole purpose for being! Whether we accept this or not, it does seem that the best thing you can do in this life is live up to your potential in as many areas as possible. You will not do this if you allow your potential to be undermined by somebody else's influence. Of course the converse applies too: you should not use your influence to subvert another's potential either.

In an ideal world, everyone would respect these views. As we know, this is not an ideal world (yet!), so we need to maintain these boundaries to limit the often-unconscious attacks against our ideas and needs.

This is "good" selfishness. Although we put emphasis on ourselves and what we need or desire, we do not do so for self enrichment at the expense of others; diverting them from fulfilling their potential. "Bad" selfish has a ruthless undercurrent; it is uncaring about the effect self-interest has upon others.

This is one of the greatest challenges for parents. Helping the children gain the emotional, psychological, and spiritual tools to help them reach their full potential without either stunting that process, or imposing our often limiting beliefs upon them.

It is a delicate line to be walked. We must pursue our potential on one side; yet avoid upsetting the journey of others in achieving theirs.

It is impossible to change others;
yet simple to transform ourselves.

It begins with the decision.

We need to want the change enough
to take the necessary steps;
to persevere.

Perhaps with a pint of patience.

PART THREE

<u>The Transformation</u>

Whether a baby or an adult,
the first steps are the hardest.
But for any journey, any life,
those first few steps are essential.

Into the needed unknown;
  leaving the familiar behind
    ...the excuses,
      ...the crutches,
        ...the justifications.

A vision of the rainbow ahead.

· 25 ·

HOW DO WE GET THERE

You may well be asking at this stage: "All of this is interesting, but what does it actually do for me? How can I use this to improve my life and become happier?"

Well this is where we talk about the "how."

I fervently believe that the mind is immensely powerful and capable of bringing about enormous improvements in the lives of those who make the effort to use this awesome tool. There are countless examples of seemingly (and medically) hopeless cases miraculously turning around and healing completely. I have personally seen people's lives change through the awesome power of their minds.

To restate an important consideration touched on earlier: You will not be able to change yourself and your life *overnight*. It will happen faster for some than for others, but does take some perseverance. Taking the first step—making the decision to improve your lot is hugely important and sets you on the road to the happiness you desire. Hold onto that from now.

The greatest task is to chip away at all the negative programming. No matter what your age, there is considerable negative programming to overcome; but the good news is that it can be fun, and you can notice changes pretty quickly by doing a little self-checking from time to time. You need to do this because the benefits often creep up on you and you may not notice them for some time.

The process outlined here is one way to go. It is not presented as "the only way." By reading through the steps and suggestions outlined, you can get a feel for the essential ingredients and make adaptations to suit your lifestyle. It is suggested though, that you follow the process described for best results. Ultimately, your future is in your hands. Taking charge of your life is the objective.

Read through the rest of the book, and then come back here to start working through each chapter. As you read this for the first time, try not to make any judgments about it. The benefit develops from doing the exercises.

In a nutshell: first, the idea is to rediscover yourself while exercising your mind to reinforce positive memories. Then we look at life and introduce habits you can cultivate, aimed at changing the way you react to the "slings and arrows" of life: to inoculate you against them. These will also contribute in offsetting the negative balance from your past. You will begin to feel better about yourself in a number of ways. As the change escalates, you will be on your way...on your voyage of self-discovery.

∼

The best way to start is to schedule some regular time (let's call it *Self-Time*): ideally, set aside an hour or more once or twice a week. If you really cannot allocate this much time, reduce the frequency before reducing the time if this is possible. In any case, allow at least a half hour per week.

It is crucial that you make this commitment and stick to it. Make a pact with yourself. This time is sacred; there can be nothing more important to you.

Many people find it easier to find the time early in the morning before the day really starts, if possible before the household wakes up. You are less strung out at this time because the stresses of the day have not begun to affect you yet. In the evening, just before bed is not a good time because by then you are tired (you do not want to fall asleep) and still wearing the stresses of the day. I know someone who gets up at three o'clock each morning! Choose a time that suits you.

Now is as good a time as any to prepare the family for the concept of your own personal time. If you are a mother, this could be a culture shock for the family!

Also prepare yourself for the fact that *you will change*. You will not be the same person at the end of this. Be aware that some people may not like these changes. Some people may feel threatened, and want the old "you" back. This is quite likely if you want to change a lifelong habit of being pliant or manipulated by those around you. Contrary qualities do not work side-by-side.

Going back to being exactly the person you are now will not be possible; just as it is not possible to go back to being exactly the same person you were ten years ago. We change and grow. What you are going to do here is determine the direction of your growth in order to enhance your life.

Choose a place where you can be comfortable and alone, remaining undisturbed for the entire time you have allocated. If you can actually get away from things, this may be better depending on your circumstances, but it is not necessary. If you are at home, make it clear to everyone that this is your private time, and they are only to disturb you if the house is burning down—if they need your help putting the fire out!

Seriously, if it is likely that there will be a lot of noise coming from children playing, the television blaring, or the thumping bass from someone's music, make a deal with the culprits to allow you this time in peace.

You will be communicating with yourself. This may be something that you have not done for a long, long time. Distraction makes it more difficult to focus in the beginning of the process. You will be doing this regularly and it gets easier.

≈

Have a pen and paper with you. A notebook or journal is a better idea. Some tissues could be a good idea too. You could set an alarm clock so that you do not keep looking at your watch. If music does not distract you, put on something you enjoy; something that relaxes you or inspires you, will work well. For most, Heavy Metal or Gangsta Rap would not be an ideal choice, but it is completely up to you.

Lying on your bed is not the best place to do this. You should be comfortable, but not too comfortable; you do not want to fall asleep. Try a favorite chair perhaps. Put your feet up if that is easier. Do not rush through the process. If you run out of time for any of the exercises, just continue at your next *Self-Time* sitting. At the end of each session, think about how you feel. Write that down and anything else that occurs to you about this experience.

To make it easier for you, you could record yourself reading the next few chapters to play while you go through the process, hitting the pause button when appropriate.

If you prefer, there are mp3 files on the Your Life Manual web site (*www.YourLifeManual.com*) that you could download for a small fee. These have been specially recorded for you to make this process easier.

Or you could just read through each section, follow the suggested process and then move on to the next section; do what is suggested there, and so on. Having a narration to guide you through will probably be the least distracting method (particularly for chapters 26 and 29).

Be aware that merely reading the following chapters without the suggested contemplation and writing will not produce the results that you want.

It is a simple process, but you have to
take the time and make the effort.

Each chapter covers one or more bite-size subject or process. It is not essential to do one chapter for each of your *Self-Time* sessions, since you set your own time limit and your needs, situation, and process will be unique (just like you are). You might find that you can get through more than one chapter in a sitting, or you may have to spread one over two or more. Rather work through each exercise for the time that you have allocated until you finish—but with an eye on the time so that you don't start a new section with only a minute or so to go. There are suggestions of things you can do to fill in any extra available time.

∿

Finally, before you start on the first sitting, it is unlikely that any of the suggestions here will have any negative effect on you; however you are responsible for your own health and well-being, so exercise caution if you have any condition that may be exacerbated by anything in this section.

Despite the pain of growing,
children feel the most joy.

Treasure those memories.
Reclaim them, guard them,
protect and experience them.

Again and again.

· 26 ·

FIND YOUR HAPPY CHILD

*Note: If you find that the time you have allowed comes
to an end before completing this chapter, go to the section headed "Concluding this Sitting" for the last few
minutes, then when you start the next session, run
through the "Preparing for Self-Time" section again.
Subsequent sessions should be started and finished
in a similar way.*

*The more relaxed you allow yourself to be, and the
less distraction there is during this chapter's sitting,
the better your results will be. If you have difficulty,
repeat this for your next Self-Time period.*

Preparing for *Self-Time*

Take a deep breath, filling your lungs, and slowly release all
the air, emptying the lungs completely. This helps relax any
tension.

Do it again, and feel yourself relaxing. If you cannot feel
any relaxation, *imagine how you would feel* if you were relaxing
all over.

Repeat the deep breath in and out a couple more times. Allow yourself to luxuriate in the aloneness enjoying the music (or
the quiet, as the case may be) and acknowledge to yourself that
you are embarking on what will prove to be one of the most important journeys you have ever taken.

This is for you! Others will eventually benefit from this adventure of yours, but for now it is about you and you alone. If this seems selfish, realize that it is your conditioning kicking in. Remember—there is good selfishness and bad selfishness. This is the good kind.

Explore Your Being

You are here on this planet to live up to your potential. How could that not be true? In order to live up to that potential, you need to discover what it is.

Do you think you already know what this potential is? Are you pursuing it? If so, ask yourself if you are happy with your life right now; doing work you enjoy; enjoying fulfilling supportive and loving relationships; loving yourself and at peace with your lot in life. If the answer to all these is yes, you may be right – but since you are reading this book, I would guess there is still more you want from life.

One thing I know for sure is that your potential and your worth to humanity are immensely greater than you imagine them to be.

As you are sitting there, think about these things. What could your full potential be? Best parent in the world? Rocket scientist? Rock star? Nobel Peace Prize winner? Doctor? Being responsible for world peace? Write down everything that appeals to you.

Give yourself time to imagine what it would be like to be that person, those people. Take as long as you wish. Be light. Fantasize.

~

When finished with that, think about what you know you are good at, those things for which you have a particular talent. This is no time for false modesty. There is probably more than one thing. Make a list. There are things that you can do better than anyone else you know. Maybe even better than anyone else in the whole world! Write them all down. It does not matter how big or small these things are. Baking a delicious cake is just as meaningful for this process as designing a passenger jet.

Don't rush yourself. Enjoy this—it is good stuff.

∾

Move on to thinking about the things that make you happy. What makes you laugh out loud? When was the last time this happened? What makes you feel good? Comfortably warm inside? What fills your heart with joy? Remember what that feeling is like. Remember it?

If it did not touch you spontaneously as you thought about it, try to bring the feeling back for a moment. Take yourself back to recall the circumstances of that event. A time when you were so happy you could burst. Your world was good then, wasn't it? Even if it was just for a brief moment, you were content. Call back that feeling again. If you find it difficult, to contact the feeling, recall as much as you can about the experience, what was the weather like, who was there, what colors did you see, what sounds, smells?

What other time did you feel like that? Feel it again. Enjoy it. Take a while. Briefly write about these times describing the feelings. What single word would you use to describe them? Write it down and underline it!

∾

If you could do anything in this world right now, what would it be? Ignore cost, ignore skill, and ignore anything else that might hold you back in real life. Write it down.

Have you even cried at the pure beauty of something? If so, recall it. If not (maybe you are a person who does not cry), imagine what it must be like to feel so intensely about something beautiful. Once again, write it down.

Do you have a passion? Is there one thing that you enjoy above everything else? It could be a hobby, a sport, your work, or some other pastime. Maybe there are a couple of things and it is difficult to choose. What is it about this thing that you enjoy the most? It probably makes you feel good in some way. Does it fulfill you? What do you feel when you do it? Describe it to yourself. You are writing all these things down, aren't you?

Now imagine how you could take this thing about which you are passionate and turn it into a career so that you can be surrounded by it all the time. How would that work? Think about this. Could you take this passion and just do it professionally? What would it take? Is it more feasible to get involved in teaching it? Maybe start distributing or selling the equipment or other paraphernalia required for this interest. How would you be able to do it? Is there some other way? Write down whatever ideas come to you. It does not matter if the ideas are crazy, set your mind free. No one else will ever see these jottings (unless you show them to someone).

∾

Now just allow your mind to drift a little. Listen to the music or the silence. You do not need to think about anything in particular, but reflecting on the things you have been writing down would be good. Just try to *be*: keep your mind away from mundane stuff, if anything outside pops up, acknowledge the thought and then let it go, don't concentrate on any one thing. If doing this gets difficult, focus on your breathing. Keep your mind away from the past (except the good feelings you have just experienced), and keep your mind away from the future.

The only thing that matters right now is *you*—You, and *this moment*. Allow yourself a few minutes of this.

~

You are urged to begin cultivating—or rather *re*-cultivating—your sense of wonder, from today, this moment. Pick anything that occurs to you: a plant, a child, a cloud, a scene, anything.

Think of the sun's rays, and how we are *just* far enough away, to receive *just* the right strength of each wavelength, to sustain life and our planet. Think about how this thing has become what it is. The process it had to go through. What is to become of it in a few moments, days, or years from now? Think of each little step that had to be traveled in arriving at what it is now. And if one small thing had been different, it would not be exactly what it is now. Isn't it amazing? Delve into yourself until you can grasp that wonder at the simplicity, economy—and at the same time, complexity of this thing.

Now start doing this with at least one thing each day.

As you teach yourself to feel more awe at the wonders around you, your life will feel richer, more precious. You will appreciate what you have more.

Concluding this Sitting

Take one of those long deep breaths filling your lungs, hold it for a moment, and then let it out, slowly and completely emptying them.

If there is still time left, go over all the good times you have recalled and let your mind supply you with even more similar good times. Relive them in your mind, noticing all details, sights, sounds, tastes, smells, and feelings.

When it is nearly time to get back to daily life (do not give into the temptation to cut this time short, use it all!), once again allow your mind to drift over what you have done during this session, then stretch, stand up—feeling refreshed, great and invigorated!

Know that you have done well. Go and look at yourself in a mirror, smile (a nice big one), and get on with your day.

Everything in nature is
constantly in a state of change.
Nothing stays the same.

We determine the direction
of the changes within ourselves.

To grow, flourish and gain peace;
or stagnate and regret.

We decide our own fate,
by omission or *com*mission.

One way or another.

·27·

What Is, And What Will Be

Note: If you find that the time you have allowed comes to an end before completing this chapter, go to the section headed "Concluding this Sitting" for the last few minutes, then when you start the next session, run through the "Preparing for Self-Time" section again. Subsequent sessions should be started and finished in a similar way.

Preparing For *Self-Time*

Start off as you did last time with a few deep breaths, feeling any tension draining away as you release each breath. If you have trouble letting go of the tension, or feeling it melt, imagine what it would feel like if you could feel it. As you do this, briefly reflect on your last session.

Who Are You

Think about yourself now. The person you are and the person that you want to be: physically, emotionally, and spiritually.

Most of us are really a combination of several people: the person we really are (often deeply hidden from view); the person other people want us to be (parents, teachers, spouses, bosses); and the person that we think we *should* be. Now look at the person you are. Think about how much of you, is really *you*. We all take on attitudes and mannerisms from those around us, and there is nothing wrong with that, as long as they complement the person you really are.

Are there parts of you that you don't like? If there are physical features that bother you, they will either be rectified or be less problematic after working on other aspects. So forget about anything physical for now.

Are there other parts of yourself that you wish were not there? Things you would like to change? Common complaints include being quick to anger; smoking, eating, or drinking too much; too shy; too loud; feelings of guilt, hopelessness, or insecurity; feeling unworthy, alone, or scared; biting fingernails; aches or pains with no physical reason.

Without thinking about any of the concerns that pop up, make a list of all the things that concern you, writing them down against the left margin of a new page. What would you like to change about yourself? It does not matter if they seem silly or petty. This is not a time for passing judgment.

Spend as long as necessary to list all you can. We are not going to work directly on all of these now. Our aim is to identify them. Despite what you may think, these are not failings. They all have a purpose.

Spend five minutes or so focusing on the more urgent changes you would like to see. What could the purpose of that feeling or condition be? Any ideas? Bear in mind that some incarnation of fear is at the root of most (maybe all) negative emotions and psychosomatic ailments. What do you fear? Can you identify connections between any of the things listed?

Who You Will Be

Now, next to each item on the list write the positive opposite word or phrase; the quality or condition that you would like to adopt. If you listed "worthless" as one of the feelings you want to be rid of, perhaps you would write "admired," "valued," or "worthy." Try to think of the best word to describe this new quality.

When this list is complete, think of what it will be like when you have removed all these problems from your life. How much more fun will your life be?

Close your eyes and get a mental image of that "new you." It may be a visual picture like a movie; a mix of feelings, sounds and smells; or just a perception. Notice how you feel inside. How you interact with other people, family, friends, colleagues, and acquaintances, even with strangers. As you visualize this, notice how much better you now feel about yourself in those situations. Carefree. Confident. Happy.

If you do not easily feel any of this, that is okay. Imagine instead what it would be like if you *were* able to feel this way. The more detail you can visualize here, the better. Take some minutes to indulge yourself.

The next step is to come up with some statements (often called affirmations) that you can use to start the process of programming your mind to accept first the possibility, and then the reality of achieving these changes you want to make.

> *Important: As we go through designing these statements, if it seems like nonsense to your rational mind, give it a chance. With patience it works!*

The use of affirmations, in one form or another, is probably part of every self-improvement program devised to help people achieve their goals. Most top business people, and sports stars use them – anyone with hurdles to overcome will benefit by using them. They are not the solution, but they can be a big part of the solution. They work.

Criteria for writing effective affirmations, are that they must be positive; they must be written down, they must be in the present tense (as though what is desired has already come to pass); and they should be fairly short and snappy—one short sentence is best, but clarity is more important than the number of words. It will also help to include a benefit that you will receive. Some believe that there must be a deadline, a time by which you will achieve this desired state. If timing is important to you, include this too. It is important to focus on *what* you want (the goal), not *how* you will get there.

Choose the two or three most important qualities that you desire—the positive aspect on the right of the list. It does not matter whether you believe that you can actually achieve these goals.

Now taking each in turn, using the rules in the last paragraph, compose an affirmation that describes what you want. For example, suppose you suffer from severe shyness, and all you really want, is to be able to participate in public speaking contests. You chose "confident" as the positive quality you desire. You might come up with something like:

"I have complete confidence in myself and I easily express myself clearly; how ever many people are listening to me."

Look at Appendix A for a selection of general affirmations that will apply to many people. Make up your own, using these for ideas if necessary.

There is no real format for the words that are used, except that the phrase should be written in a way *you* would say it. Do not try to make your affirmation sound fancy, or use big words unless that is the way you usually think and talk. If you swear a lot, feel free to include your favorite expletive! Actually, emotive words will probably provide a turbo-boost to the affirmation.

Don't rush this stage, and try not to get frustrated. Make the affirmation as short as you can without taking any meaning away from it. Revise and refine it until you are happy that you cannot improve it. This process of arriving at exactly the right phrase serves the purpose of embedding the positive objective in your mind, so it is not time wasted. Now each time you read it or say it, it has more impact.

When you have finished your two or three affirmations, write that final version of each onto a fresh page of your journal. Read the first one aloud five times. Each time, put the emphasis in a

different place. The fifth time; put enthusiastic emotion into it.
Now read through the rest of them in the same way.

∼

Before continuing, add one more affirmation. Feel free to change the words a bit, but if you are tempted to water it down, making yourself seem less special, rather use it exactly as written here.

Here it is: *"I am a unique, wonderful and special person worthy of giving and receiving love; I have unique talents and abilities to offer the world. I deserve genuine happiness."*

Change the word "person" to woman, man, boy or girl; whichever applies to you.

You should read your affirmations (or even better, memorize and recite them) as often as possible. Aloud if there are no people around to look at you strangely!

Put enthusiasm into your delivery and gesticulate if that is in your nature. A good time for this is when you are driving alone, stopped at a traffic light or while waiting for something.

Whatever you do, make a point of repeating them each two or three times, first thing in the morning, and again last thing at night before bed. It is not necessary to think about the aim of the affirmations or how you will reach it. Nor is an emotive recitation essential, but it adds impetus to the process.

There are a number of things that you can do to make it easier to keep your affirmations available. Print them out on a card that you can keep in your purse or wallet with driver's license or credit cards, or stick them on the fridge with some magnets. Or if you read a lot, print them on a nice bookmark to remind you each time you start and stop reading. If you are a computing genius, make up a screen-saver slide show of them, or desktop wallpaper. Use your imagination to keep them in your mind.

You could also further develop the most important affirmation into a two or three word mantra* you can repeat to yourself dozens of times a day.

∾

If there is still time before this session ends, think about how you will feel when the changes covered by your affirmations have come to pass. Allow your mind to drift over what you have done during this *Self-Time*. You have started the ball rolling!

∾

Persevere with the affirmations even if it seems that they are not doing any good. Realize that anyone who says affirmations don't work, in all likelihood, merely gave up too soon to reap the benefits.

There is little effort involved in repeating them and they *will* work—but it takes a while and at first the changes are subtle; they sneak up on you. One day you will suddenly realize that there has been a shift inside you. For now, trust your mind.

Concluding this Sitting

When there are a few minutes left, take another of those deep breaths, filling your lungs, and let it out slowly, completely emptying them. Let your mind drift over what you have just been doing.

Stretch, smile to yourself, and get back to your day; once again feeling refreshed, wonderful, enthusiastically invigorated!

---

*   The Sanskrit word mantra is used in Eastern religions but is often used in the West to refer to a series of repeated words, like a slogan, without any religious connotations.

· 28 ·

REFINEMENT AND ANALYSIS

Note: The comments preceding the last two chapters about matching available time to chapter content continue to apply.

Preparing For *Self-Time*

Start off this sitting as before – take a few of those deep breaths, feeling all stress slipping away as you slowly, completely release each breath. Go over your affirmations again. If it has been some days since your last session, they are probably pretty familiar by now.

Another Look At Your Affirmations

Today we will be looking at the affirmations that you composed. If you have found that the actual phrases that you decided on last time do not really resonate with you as well as you thought they would, we will be looking at the wording again later.

Pick one of the affirmations and read it out loud to yourself. Think again about what it means to you. Close your eyes and construct a mental picture of yourself at some time in the future when the aim of this affirmation will have been fulfilled. As mentioned previously, this may be visual, sensory, or whatever else suits your imaginative process. Each person imagines things in their own way.

Consider how you will feel and your interaction with any-one else who will be affected by your transformation. Will your outlook on life be different? Will family and friends be as happy with this new you as you are? Is there a downside? Think care-fully about this.

Everything has side effects; sometimes these are good, other times, they are not. Getting promoted means more money, but also more responsibility and possibly longer hours spent at work. Finding love and marriage brings fulfillment, but also reduces personal freedom of action and means added responsibility. Win-ning the lottery makes you rich, but it can also reduce security and make you wonder about people's motives.

Usually the price is one worth paying, but it is wise to con-sider the price of anything before making the purchase!

Now think about the changes that will have to take place for you to reach your desired goal. There will probably have to be changes within you. There is no need to be concerned about *how* those changes will take place, just *what* the changes will be. Follow those changes and look for a root change; the one altera-tion that will flow through and facilitate the specific transfor-mation you desire. The root may be the first thing that occurs to you, or it may take several steps to find it. Write down each one in your journal.

Taking the earlier example of a desire to overcome shyness and take part in public speaking: from the affirmation, we know that more confidence is necessary. Asking what will bring this about would probably end up with a root change that would require improved self-esteem. Usually the changes we desire in ourselves have their root in a self-esteem deficiency. Virtually every one of us could do with a good dose of extra self-respect.

When you reach this root change, ask whether you are com-fortable with this change. Realize that this change will also affect other parts of your life. If you gain self-esteem and more confi-dence, the change will not only reflect in your public speaking;

but it will radiate throughout your life touching everything. Some people feel threatened or intimidated in the face of confidence, so relationships could be affected.

This is not usually a significant problem; however if there is a downside to transforming our lives, it is likely because we have not anticipated the consequential changes that inevitably ensue.

If you could wave a magic wand right now and have this transformation occur, would you do it?

Now expand your view out to those around you. Who, other than you, will be most affected by your change? Consider the root change as well as the desired result and other likely consequences. It could be that this person is actually encouraging you on your way. If so, that is good; but do you think they realize the extent of the transformation?

People are generally comfortable with the world they know. We do not like change, perhaps it is because we subconsciously know that there are many dimensions to any change, many of which are not anticipated. People do not change in isolation. Change has a ripple effect. Many feel challenged by change and resent it. If you feel the "new, improved you" will not be completely embraced, you must do some careful thinking to determine your plan of action.

You could just say that you have your life to live and will deal with anything that crops up when (and if) it happens. Ultimately it is your choice, but avoiding conflict is a good thing. It is also good to exercise your mind, and this process does just that!

Try to figure out what reaction you will receive, and the reason for it. By knowing where it comes from, it may be possible for you to anticipate and alleviate the cause before any unpleasantness arises.

If the response is likely to be anything other than complete acceptance, this is probably the best solution. First prize here would be for this to turn out to be a positive growth experience for all concerned!

The remaining alternatives are to go ahead and accept that your metamorphosis could end the relationship; or to make the choice not to pursue your transformation in the interests of harmony.

Neither of these is desirable. Unless a relationship is fundamentally flawed, as in the case of abuse, every effort should be made to maintain it. The harmony sought in the last option may end up being short-lived since you would be suppressing your desire for change.

The purpose of going through this thinking process is to anticipate stumbling blocks and ensure that your objective is worth the price.

Now go through any other people that will be affected in the same way as you have just done with the person most affected.

When finished with this, it is likely that you will be just as motivated to continue your transformation, and have a plan (even if just a rough idea) of how to keep your important relationships sound.

Now go on to your next affirmation and follow the same process for each of them.

∾

You may have discovered in your musing that the wording which you so carefully chose previously is not quite right. Perhaps you feel that the flavor needs to be changed slightly. Feel free to make changes now, fine tuning until you are happy with each one; but don't keep changing them every day or so. It is the repetition that makes them so powerful.

As time goes by, as the changes start, you will probably feel the need to retune the affirmations slightly in order to focus them more specifically. This is good, and changes must be made to keep the affirmations focused.

When you are happy with any revisions, write them all again on a new page of your journal. Spend a few more minutes repeating each one four or five times. They will be even more powerfully loaded in your mind now.

You know what you want, have a good idea of the effects it will generate and how you will turn it all into a favorable result. You still have no real idea how it will happen, but your subconscious is working on that twenty-four hours a day. You needn't second-guess that process.

Concluding this Sitting

When it is time to stop, allow yourself to relax. Close your eyes for a moment. Take one of those deep breaths, filling your lungs, and let it out slowly, and completely.

Stretch your arms, legs and back. Smile. Then get on with your day, Sparkling!

Back in the late seventies, I attended a management training workshop. There we watched a film (this was before video) entitled "Time To Think".

The point of the movie was illustrating that with all the hustle and bustle of life, and all the demands on our time—the noise has increased significantly since then—the only way to arrive at effective decisions is to claim a little peace, time to reflect upon the choices open to us. Time to think.

This training movie was specifically aimed at teaching management and supervisory staff that taking the time and the space necessary to make the right decision would pay off in the long run, even though the situation may be hectic.

The lesson of this way of thinking is just as sound in our personal lives. We need to make time to think about our choices. Weigh the pros and cons. Block out the noise. Have some quiet time. Take time to think.

· 29 ·

Personal Quiet Time

Preparing For *Self-Time*

To start off this session, once again take a few of those deep breaths, feeling yourself becoming calmer as you slowly and completely release each breath.

Close your eyes and run through your affirmations again. Keep up with them daily, making them a regular habit.

Quiet Meditation

Today we are going to work on a form of meditation. Some people have strong feelings about meditation, so we will discuss it a little before continuing.

If you are comfortable and familiar with meditation already, you can skip the next few paragraphs.

If you baulk at the thought of trying it because of things you may have read or been told, try to put those impressions aside for now and read on.

There is nothing sinister about what we are suggesting you do here. Although there is no direct religious or mystical significance, most religions have some form of meditation although it is sometimes called something else—it is a component of prayer, for example.

Interestingly, scientific research has revealed that the prayer of Franciscan nuns and the meditation of Buddhist monks result in very much the same brain activity*.

By meditating as described in this chapter, the aim is to reach a point where you are able to remove distraction to contemplate your being effectively.

There are so many things going on in our lives from moment to moment, and so much that we have to remember and attend to, it is difficult to clear all the clutter that goes on in our heads. This chaotic state stops us from really considering anything objectively.

There is no message attached to this proceeding. There are no religious overtones, although it must be said that sometimes people do receive religious or spiritual insights—but these enhance their existing belief system. Done regularly, meditation will help you to make better decisions and be far clearer about your purpose.

Read through the description that follows on the next page and you will see that it is really quite simple, although it takes a bit of practice to master.

∾

As mentioned, our purpose for meditating is to remove distraction and mind-clutter. To do this, you should be wearing loose-fitting clothes, and be comfortable. You could be sitting on the floor in the lotus position if you wish, but this is not necessary and is quite uncomfortable if you are not used to it!

It is best to sit on the floor or in a chair with your back straight so that you do not slouch and constrict your breathing. Before starting, decide when you wish to finish meditating. With enough practice you will be aware when it is time to stop without using

---

* For more: "Why God Won't Go Away: Brain Science and the Biology of Belief" by Andrew Newberg and Eugene G. d'Aquili with Vince Rause. Ballantine Books, 2002.

a clock or watch, but do not expect that yet. For this first time, allow five or ten minutes.

~

Take a few slow, deep breaths, just as you have been doing at the beginning of each *Self-Time* sitting, being sure to expel all the air as you breathe out. This improves oxygenation of your blood and reduces tension.

Now, breathing naturally, look for something a comfortable distance away at about eye level: a plant, or a spot on the wall perhaps. Now still looking at that point, shift your eye's focus to a point slightly closer to you so that you see shapes, but nothing distinct. This is called "soft focus." There should be no eyestrain and you should blink regularly as you usually do.

Being aware that there are no rules regarding this meditation— and whatever you do or experience will be worthwhile, move your mind's focus to your breathing. Be aware of each breath. Feel the breath moving in through your nose, down through the back of your throat, your windpipe and on to your lungs. Here, it quickly swaps oxygen for carbon dioxide, and reverses direction flowing back until it is breathed out through your nose or mouth.

Keep your mind focused on each breath, without anticipating the next one, nor thinking of the last. Let your mind release itself from each breath as it flows out of your body. Counting each breath in and then out is a common method of maintaining this "present time" focus, feeling any sensations that accompany the breathing.

When anything other than your mindful breathing crops up (and it will!), acknowledge it; then let it go. If you get a sudden itch that demands scratching, acknowledge it, let it go, and get back to your breathing. Scratching that itch will not make it go away, just make it come back again, perhaps in a different place. In a way, you are disciplining your mind to allow you this time. We are not used to "doing nothing," so your body and mind, not understanding what is going on, tries to give you something to do.

Recognizing a feeling or thought, then purposefully dismissing it to be taken up at a later time, is a skill that becomes easier with time and practice. For now, do the best you can, then move back to the breathing focus.

Whatever happens, do not get frustrated. This is all part of the process. You will probably be acknowledging and dismissing thoughts virtually the whole time for the first few times you meditate. You will suddenly become aware of an itch, or thoughts about something that happened earlier. Persevere. As you become aware of these distractions, just get back to your breathing focus.

~

In time, you may find that you suddenly feel detached from everything around you. It does not happen to everyone, and whether it happens or not is not a sign of success or failure. It can be quite a surprise when it first happens, but it is quite normal, and should be welcomed. In this state you are more likely to experience sudden clarity of vision or purpose, but there are benefits you will reap even if this never happens to you.

What happens, happens; what doesn't, doesn't. There is no right. There is no wrong.

As time goes by, with this regular quiet time, you will find yourself becoming less bothered by those things that you cannot control, less stressed, more relaxed. You may begin to realize that things which you used to think were so important, no longer are. It will become easier to let go of things that illogically used to consume you.

Once you have finished your first meditation period of five or ten minutes think of how it went. Were you distracted a lot, or were you able to focus fairly easily? The odds are that you probably had some trouble. Were there sudden itches, maybe thoughts that would not go away? None of these matter. It was time well spent. Just as the benefits of affirmations sneak up on you, so do the benefits of meditation.

It has been known for thousands of years that personal quiet time is important and beneficial: turning off the noise of life for a moment. Do yourself an enormous favor and resist any thoughts that tell you this is a waste of time, it is not working, or any other negative idea that prompts you to give up.

If you can find half an hour to an hour each day, or even just a few times a week to practice meditation, that would be wonderful. In any case, from now on, any time you end up with spare time during your *Self-Time* sessions before your allotted time is up, spend the remaining minutes meditating.

∾

For the rest of the time available for this sitting, review in your mind what you have done over the past four chapters. You have rediscovered some of your happiest moments; worked out what you would like to change in your life; what your desired qualities/attributes are; the effect this will have on your life and those close to you; composed specific individual affirmations; and practiced being in the present moment. Recall each of these stages, and how you felt about each one.

Examine yourself mentally: do you notice any small positive changes in your outlook, or attitudes? If you do, enjoy the realization. If not, don't be concerned. Change takes time and persistence. Keep at it and the changes will happen soon enough.

Concluding this Sitting

When the time is up, allow yourself to relax. Take a deep breath, filling your lungs, and let it out slowly, and completely.

Stretch slowly and get on with your day, smiling and sparkling.

*One of the main differences
between leaders in any field
and the average person-in-the-street,
is their ability to focus on
the matter at hand—
excluding all non-related
peripheral concerns
and distractions.*

· 30 ·

Parking Problems

*Note: From here on, continue to start and finish each
of your sittings with the deep breathing and relaxation
exercises with which you are now familiar.*

*Remember too, to continue making notes of relevant
points and whatever else occurs to you during these
sessions. These notes further embed information into
your subconscious mind. It is particularly powerful
because you are thinking it while you are writing it.
It is like using a double-barreled shotgun!*

Obsessions

As you read, think of your life and notice any similarities.
Consciously exercise your mind.

Do you sometimes find yourself becoming obsessed by something that you just cannot let go? It may even be that it overtakes your life for a while. You may keep speaking about it perhaps, examining different aspects, going around in circles.

It could be something fairly inconsequential, like turning the house upside down in an attempt to find some object you remember from some time past. At other times it could be far more emotionally charged, like constantly thinking about a loved one or a pet that has died, perhaps some guilt or regret over things never said or done.

Or it could be that you feel slighted by somebody and this prevents you from moving on as you fume over her words or actions.

Some are affected by obsessions like these more than others, but everyone experiences them at times.

A common thread running through all of these is that of repeated negative imprinting. Each time you think about the cause of this emotion, it reinforces the initial feeling. Based on the examples given, the feelings could be incompetence, grief, guilt, regret, anger, and helplessness. What others can you think of? Whatever the specifics, they are negative, and that is something we do not need.

Many times, the feeling that engenders this negative effect is perfectly normal and is part of a natural process, whether it involves grief, or the primal fight/flight instincts awakened by confrontation. The focus during this chapter is not to debate the appropriateness of the feeling, but to explore your reaction to it.

Think for a while about things in your own life. Can you recall times in your life that fall into this category of obsessive, repeated negative imprints? They may be similar to the examples mentioned, or totally different. They may take the form of a grudge against someone that preoccupies you. This is the main indicator: repeated, negative preoccupation with something: an inability to let go and move on.

Compartmentalization

One way to get out of this pattern is to use compartmentalization. This trick is very effective in stopping your mind from perpetuating the negative imprints.

We can look at your mind as one of those pigeonhole mail and message boards that used to be very common in hotels and offices before e-mail and instant messaging flourished. What we do is simply to place the offending thoughts into one of the pigeonholes, leaving it there to be dealt with at a later time.

We are not getting rid of it, nor are we forgetting about it, or burying it. You could say we are parking the problem, to be handled later. This is a conscious choice that is made to attend to a problem at a more convenient time: it is *not* an escape. It is important to recognize this.

There are two main advantages to using compartmentalization. First, it allows you to move on and function without being constantly distracted. Second, while the problem is parked, your subconscious mind is busily working on it in the background so that when you return to it later, a lot (if not all) of the fire has gone out of it and you are able to attend to it in a more rational manner.

An added bonus of mastering this ability is that the process works well in general problem solving too. Because of its many uses, this is a skill well worth developing. It takes practice and time to acquire it and apply it properly, but the time and effort is worthwhile.

Have you ever wondered how the leaders of countries and huge corporations manage to keep themselves from becoming overwhelmed by each new problem and crisis? It is because they have mastered the skill of compartmentalization (parking problems) that they are able to attend to each new crisis as though the others do not exist.

At the outset you need to work with less trying issues before attempting to park more serious problems.

Depending upon how many affirmations you are using, you may like to compose another one about a new ability you have to park problems easily and effectively so your subconscious can assist in finding solutions while you deal with other matters.

∾

This learned skill of parking thoughts, feelings, or problems begins with a decision to "remove yourself" from them. You do this by acknowledging that the feeling exists, and choosing to park it (you can use whatever term you choose) for the time being. This cannot be stressed too much: *it is most important not to deny the problem or pretend that it does not exist.* This is where it is easy to go wrong.

Next, consciously move your focus onto something else. It could be something that you need to attend to, or even just a more pleasant thought or memory. This is the difficult part when you are first practicing the technique. It is difficult to keep your mind away from the unpleasant feeling, particularly if you do not catch it early in the process. Remember that each time you allow yourself to be distracted; you are reinforcing the negative effect. This makes it more difficult to remove yourself from the issue. With physical ailments, early detection assists in effective treatment. Compartmentalization works the same way.

You will be more effective at parking the problems easily if you make the choice to park them as soon as you become aware that you are becoming consumed by nagging or obsessive thoughts. It may seem like too much trouble to develop this skill, particularly if you first try it when hit by a dire situation.

To use another analogy, we spend much time learning new skills: training our bodies until they are at peak physical fitness, learning to play a game well, or a musical instrument; yet we spend little time training our minds to become mentally fit. This mental fitness will be addressed in more detail later.

As you practice and develop this skill, you will become more proficient at early identification and effective compartmentalization of fixations and problems.

Remember to keep on with the affirmations and your quiet time. Persistence and perseverance pay off!

· 31 ·

POSITIVE AND NEGATIVE;
GOOD AND BAD

Imbalance

Now a topic you have already encountered frequently here: positive and negative influences and experiences.

Do you know the negative things that are influencing your life most today? What about the positive? Is there anything that you can practically do to reduce that negative for today? And what can you do to increase the effect of the most positive factor? Overall, which would you judge to be more dominant so far today: positive, or negative?

Whichever way you answered this last question, you *do* have an overall "positive deficiency." We all do.

There is an endless list of small things that we can do to increase our daily dose of positive input. We will look at a few here, but this subject never ends and we will touch on others later. Time taken to devise other more personally specific methods would be well spent.

Regular deep breathing, like the way you start your *Self-Time* sessions, helps to raise the spirits. There are health spin-offs too, increasing oxygenation, blood flow, and improving your heart rate—so it is worth developing a habit of doing this several times a day. If you ever feel down about something, make a point of breathing deeply a few times.

Good And Bad

Nothing that happens is inherently good or bad. What makes it one or the other is merely your reaction to it. All things are really neutral, or looking at it from a different perspective, they contain elements of both good and bad.

This concept is understandably difficult to accept when we consider examples of terror and all the horrific things that humans can do to each other. Here is a true story of what happened to a South African insurance broker in 1994:

Two men abducted Alison outside her home in Port Elizabeth and raped her. Then they disemboweled her by stabbing her so many times that doctors could not count the wounds. Then to make sure that she would not survive, they slashed her throat sixteen times, eventually leaving her for dead out in a clearing, in the middle of nowhere. Determined to survive, Alison dragged herself to a road, collapsing across a white arrow painted on the surface. Eventually a passing motorist found her and rushed her to a hospital where the staff were amazed that she was still alive. Alison survived and later faced her attackers in court.

The story does not end here. Refusing to allow this traumatic emotional and physical ordeal to destroy her life, Alison turned this terrible experience into a positive, inspirational triumph over unimaginable odds.

Alison is now a sought after motivational speaker. Describing how she has dealt with the challenges of her experience, she has become an example for both women and men around the world*. She is now married, with a son born in 2003.

> *No matter what happens in life - we always get to choose what we're going to do with it.*
>
> ~ *Alison*

---

* For more on Alison's story, see "I Have Life – Alison's Journey" as told to Marianne Thamm, available from www.alison.co.za

Was Alison's experience bad? Looking at the attack in isolation, yes it was. Looking at the whole story, only Alison can judge whether it was or not. Was it negative? No.

Alison took what would have destroyed most of us and turned it into a life enriching opportunity, even helping survivors of the 9/11 tragedy.

Alison's story illustrates that good can come out of extreme adversity. It was her attitude to the event that made the difference between it being a positive or negative situation.

Balancing Act

Often those weakened by the effect of a veritable avalanche of negative experience will feel the situation is hopeless, that there is no way out. It stands to reason in a predicament like this that escape will be more complicated than in a less severe case, however the process would essentially be the same although more arduous.

Awareness of the effect of a negative balance is in itself useful, but there are practical steps that can be taken to minimize the negative impact of daily life. If we wish to level the balance (or better, shift it the other way), it is essential to take active steps to make it happen.

One approach is to eliminate or reduce your exposure to negative influence; another is to emphasize the positive influences.

Some find that canceling the newspaper subscription and avoiding television news makes a significant difference. There is far more bad news reported than good; and while each story may not directly affect us, the cumulative effect does.

The most extreme adjustment would be removing oneself from the major source of negativity: if a man physically or mentally abuses his partner and will not change, it may be in her best interest to leave him.

This example by no means suggests that we should run away from our problems. Relationships require work. The effort expended developing a respectful, loving friendship contributes to building the strongest bonds. However when one person in a relationship is only interested in personal gratification at the expense of the other, happiness is difficult to achieve. If the selfish partner does not value the relationship sufficiently and refuses to adjust to a mutually acceptable degree, extreme measures may be necessary. In most instances though, such drastic change is usually avoidable.

Arriving at the right sources of negativity to excise depends on the individual. What are the things that push your negative buttons? What upsets you that you can do without? You may intuitively know what to get rid of, or you may actively *need to feel* the effects of events in your life to determine the main culprits.

Fake it 'til you make it

Whatever you think of yourself, you are *so much more than that*! You really *are* capable of more than you have ever imagined. To use a favorite phrase of Deepak Chopra's your potential is brim full of *infinite possibilities*! Whatever you decide to achieve, you can achieve. The only limits are those you place on yourself.

For most people, the greatest positive change can be achieved by altering our interaction with people, the world around us, and the way we look at ourselves. Luckily, we can begin by just *pretending* that we feel the way that we want to feel. You will notice the change quite quickly, and soon you will not have to pretend anymore.

There is no magic involved in this; it is an old motivational technique. Our minds are immensely powerful. We can psych ourselves into achieving anything that we desire just by wanting it, and pretending to ourselves that we already have it. If you do not believe this, it is your negative programming fooling you!

Professional sports stars use this process, so do business leaders. Although these are leaders in their field, it does not take a leader to master the same techniques. Actually it could be said that in order to have reached the level they have, they probably mastered the process of positive reinforcement. All it takes is some diligence and patience—Persistence.

You will soon notice small changes, build it into a habit, and become a believer in the power of positive thought.

~

The best way to start this process, is to stop putting yourself down in any way. Stop verbalizing anything derogatory about yourself. Even if you know the comments you used to make about yourself are not true—that they are merely light-hearted (but untrue) observations, refrain!

And, if by any chance you *do* believe the negative comments, then *definitely* stop making them!

Remember, you have a net balance of negative self-esteem in your mind. Your mind does not consider the truth of what is said. In the absence of contradictory "facts" it accepts what it receives as being true, without critical judgment—particularly when it comes from a trusted source and more so when emphatic or emotional. And whom would your mind trust more than you?

Everything negative that you say (and to a slightly lesser extent, think) about yourself reinforces the negative balance. Similarly, everything positive that you say has a neutralizing effect on the negative. As you chip away at the negatives, the increasing positives affect you more and more positively. It is really just like arithmetic: pluses and minuses arriving at a positive or negative result.

Often, when you meet with someone and ask how she is, you receive a noncommittal response like, "Okay." Or a little worse, "Not so bad." Depending on how it is said the first could be negative. The second example definitely is. We should avoid ambiguous and negative responses.

A little part of you will believe it if you respond: "Terrific, thanks, are you doing well too?" Or even just, "Great, thanks!" Emphasize that first word. It does not matter whether you have a headache. Most of the time, the person asking is not really that interested anyway. Use the opportunity to build a bit of positive input for both of you!

Probably because of our learned aversion to boasting, we can also find ourselves falling into the habit of making remarks that diminish the real impact of our achievements.

When we receive a compliment, we may play down the attribute or accomplishment, or even deny it completely. Instead of politely acknowledging the compliment, we throw it back at them—perhaps feeling guilty about being smart, or pretty, or lucky, enough to stand out from the crowd.

Pride in itself is not a sin. Being overly proud and using it as a weapon to overshadow or belittle others could be considered a sin: it certainly is not an attractive behavior. Carrying on about our accomplishments, giving the impression that we hold ourselves above others is also not likely to win friends.

Humble pride is good and worthy; it helps tremendously to build up positivity. Be proud of accomplishments (whatever they are) then try to keep them to yourself unless someone else compliments you; then acknowledge gratefully and carry on with life.

Celebrate your achievements. Congratulate yourself. Take every opportunity to boost the positive! Boost your own accomplishments, as well as those of people around you.

People like you more when you praise them; they are more likely to help you enhance your positivity too… it is catching.

Another positive activity that can revitalize our lives is more smiling. Try smiling briefly at everyone with whom you make eye contact. It will brighten the circle around you and have a positive impact on your own disposition.

A little imagination and knowledge of your personal positive and negative buttons is bound to generate other methods of accentuating the positive and minimizing the negative in your life.

Become consciously aware of your reaction to whatever happens. When you feel a negative charge from something, try to find the positive. This can be difficult, but part of the solution is always to be aware of what you are feeling. Even so, sometimes we are too close to the action to see the whole picture.

This concept is part of the main theme of this book, so we are not done with all this yet!

While learning sales techniques years ago, I was encouraged to use what my trainer called "Hollywood Glitz" words. These are the words that are used to promote Hollywood movies. Usually these will be words that are not commonly in day-to-day use or are not used in their usual context. The purpose of this is to surprise the listener, get attention, and generate an attractive impression or illusion.

A favorite expression in sales and marketing is to "sell the sizzle, not the steak." In other words, use sensory words rather than common descriptive words. Using the steak example, talk about the smell (tantalizing, wafting), the sound (sizzling, crackling), the taste (delectable, juicy), the texture (succulent, melt-in-the-mouth) and the atmosphere (inviting, warm, hot), rather than describing a searing lump of decaying meat.

A creative friend once signed off his emails with the phrase "Kool Bananas!" we were really amused by this and still use the phrase from time to time to emphasize that something is particularly enticing.

Emotive words carry more impact, whether the recipient is a friend, a customer, colleague...or your mind.

Sparkle! Shimmer! Scintillate!

· 32 ·

No Limits

The Power Of Belief

Do you sometimes quit doing something because you feel you don't have the ability to do whatever it is? Do you often have that feeling? How about a feeling of inferiority? Is there someone who makes you feel incapable of doing things properly?

If you answered, "yes" to any or all of these questions, read on. We will look at ways to analyze why this is so. Even if you said, "no" to all of them, read on anyway.

Most of us are able to do most of what we really want to do. This is worth repeating: *Most of us are able to do most of what we really want to do.* This is certain.

It is probable that we are *all* able to do *whatever* we really want to do. What restricts us from doing anything we desire, are the self-defeating limitations that we place upon ourselves.

If you believe that you cannot do something, you are right. But it is only the *belief* that restricts you, not some boundary to your innate ability. The power that belief has over our minds is a blessing, but sometimes its effectiveness works against us too.

If you believe something, your mind unquestioningly accepts it to be true. Since your mind is what provides you with both confidence and self-doubt, your beliefs are crucial.

≈

I have led a varied life, doing many different jobs in completely different fields, having many hobbies and pastimes over the years. So far, I have not found anything that I cannot do. I have certainly felt the fear of entering the unknown, doing something new, but that fear does not last.

Most people are not geniuses; successful people (however success is measured) just apply their minds to a fairly narrowly defined area of expertise. A single person did not design the space shuttle; it took a team of thousands, each with a particular specialty. Whatever it is that *you* do all day, you do the same thing, but probably with less publicity and glamour attached to the result.

It is unfortunate that society places more value on some occupations than others, however being a teacher, mother, or father should really be rated more highly that being a rocket scientist or a rock star.

The thing that prevents most people from taking a chance, doing what they really want to do, is the apparent enormity of that task, or change.

Most complex tasks are best approached in a structured, methodical way. One effective way to do this is to break the task or problem into manageable chunks. Make a list of each of these chunks and decide the most efficient order each task should be completed. Then you can determine what is required to accomplish each step. It is much easier, and less intimidating to get started by focusing on these smaller more manageable bits. As each small task is completed, move onto the next. Like doing a jigsaw puzzle, eventually this sequence of completed small pieces grows into the whole.

For most of us humans, there are a few things that we simply do not seem able to grasp. With proper teaching, it might be possible to overcome these apparent limitations, but it is unlikely that we will ever be required to master the physics that Stephen Hawking uses to explain theories of the creation of the Universe.

Undue Influence

Unfortunately, you might find that some other person makes a point of accentuating each and every perceived deficiency in things you do, undermining your confidence. Like all destructive criticism of this kind, this attitude is more about the other person than it is about you. Often it will have a root in feelings of inadequacy in some area, a need to divert attention from their shortcomings by focusing on yours.

If you are in this position, look at your critic. Perhaps you can figure out what is driving their criticism and take steps to neutralize it. Each situation is different, so generalizing is dangerous, but boosting the other person's self-esteem might be all that is required. A deeper understanding of what motivates this criticism can, in itself, be helpful to you in neutralizing the effect that it has on you.

Challenge Yourself

A good way to overcome these self-defeating demons is to challenge yourself. Think of something that you would really like to do; perhaps a task that you are uncertain to take on because you don't know how well you'll be able to do it. It could be starting a new hobby, taking on added responsibility at work, learning something that you know nothing about or moving to a new neighborhood. Take up painting, carpentry, rock climbing, archery, or bungee jumping. It does not matter what it is, but it should preferably not be life threatening at this stage! For the process to be meaningful, it must be something reasonably complex to do, requiring more than a simple decision to do it. It is important that it must be something that you *want* to do.

Now figure out what you need to make it happen. Make a list of things you will need to do. Answer questions like who you will need to contact for more information?

Do you need to gather facts about this thing from the library or Internet? Will you need any special equipment or clothing?

What other steps are necessary? You could end up with just a few items, or a long list.

Once you speak to someone about it, you may have to add more items to the list. Now work out the order in which you want to tackle the items on the list, bearing in mind that some items may depend on others being completed beforehand. No matter how long the list is, take the first point and work on that without concerning yourself with the steps that follow. As a simple example, if your plan is to take up oil painting, don't worry about applying the paint correctly before actually arriving at the studio to learn, because you will be taught then anyway.

Any time you start to feel out of your depth when starting something new, tell yourself that it is perfectly normal to feel this way, that you are perfectly capable, and the distress will pass as you gain knowledge and experience. You are able and worthy.

If you never seem to be able to do anything right—and a huge part of the population feels this way—there is a way to break out of this prison. Perhaps you feel this way because there is (or was) someone close who keeps telling you how useless you are, picking apart whatever you do; or perhaps you have just found that, over time, whatever you do somehow always seems to go wrong.

If you identify with this description, at some point you started to doubt your ability. Once that happened, you began tasks with a negative expectation.

You may have said to yourself, "I will probably not do this right." Or, "I hope I don't fail." Or, "I don't know if I can,"

And each time you fail, it becomes easier to succeed at failing, and to accept each failure too, because: "…that is just the way I am."

You may have justified this attitude to yourself by saying that you are just being realistic. Perhaps you say that you are pessimistic because: "…if I fail, I won't be disappointed; but if I succeed, I will be pleasantly surprised."

As we have discovered, the mind is immensely powerful.

Each time you allow yourself to expect results less than those you wish, you are setting yourself up to fail. This then becomes what has been dubbed "a self fulfilling prophecy." Subconsciously, you make it happen!

If we can make this happen, we can just as easily make the opposite happen too.

Realize though, that by its very nature, succeeding takes more effort than failure. But now, instead of expecting failure, you can expect success. It takes a mind shift and a fair amount of repetition to overcome the failure habit.

People who are known as "accident prone" suffer from the same syndrome, believing that they were born that way and there is nothing they can do about it. This is nonsense.

Reinforcing Intention

So, from today, any time you feel inadequate or prone to failure, tell yourself that you are able to do anything that you choose to do. Whenever you look at yourself in the mirror, tell your reflection this: "I am able to do anything I choose to do. I do not place limits on myself or on my abilities." Even add this as one of your affirmations.

Naturally, this does not mean that you should decide to jump out of a window and fly! It does not mean that you give yourself carte blanche to step on anyone who gets in your way, either!

When you begin anything where you would have doubted your ability in the past, now remind yourself that despite a little doubt (which is natural), you *are* capable, and you *will* succeed. In fact, that slight doubt will give you an edge by reminding you never to allow those self-defeating thoughts to take over again.

As soon as you become aware of the emergence of any self-defeating thoughts, banish them with reminders of the new successful you. You are creating the syndrome of success!

In New Age circles, there is much talk about the "power of intention." In other words, this means *how to get what you want.*

Many processes and techniques are described for harnessing this power, but they all seem to boil down to the three things: Define what you want; visualize having it in detail; meditate or think about it, often using affirmations.

This power does exist. It has been used successfully for decades, possibly longer, although it is often called goal setting or motivation. Words of warning though, bear in mind the maxim: "Be careful what you wish for."

· 33 ·

THE WORLD AS YOUR STAGE

*Have you noticed any positive changes yet? If so, cel-
ebrate them and congratulate yourself. If not, continue
to be patient, persevere with your affirmations. Trust
yourself. Changes will come. Look out for them.
Find some time to review your previous* Self-Time
*sessions. Recall the visualizations from the first few
sittings, filling in as many details as you can for each.
In particular, imagine yourself being the person you
wish to be. Give your mind a workout!*

Acting And Becoming

You can use your mind to improve your life. In this chapter we
add more tools to your self-improvement toolbox.

As the Buddha said, you become what you think. Building
from that, here is another thought:

If you act it, you become it.

If your desire is to be a millionaire, this does *not* mean that
you should immediately rush out and start spending money as if
there were no limits! Millionaires do not act this way; otherwise
they would end up broke. It also does not mean that you now
start telling everyone that you are a millionaire, changing your
attitude towards family and friends.

What this phrase means, is that you should conduct yourself as if you were the person you wish to be. Using the millionaire example, you should act as though you have already developed the necessary qualities to be that millionaire.

This acting like who you wish to be refers more to acting the part internally, with feelings rather than actions. However you have pictured the "New Improved You," what are the emotional, or mindset changes that will be necessary?

A common quality that will typically be required by most people in one form or another is greater self-confidence. This could manifest itself in the wish to become more outgoing, believe more in your abilities, get a particular job, find a partner, or feel less fearful, amongst countless of other possibilities.

Acting as if you had more confidence, you will find that you actually *feel* more confident once you overcome your initial jitters. To start off, you may feel like a fraud, but don't let this stop you. Others will not notice that you are acting as long as you don't overdo it.

An Easy Start

If you are reluctant to jump off into the deep end, start with something easy. Whenever you make eye contact with someone (and the situation is appropriate!) smile at them. Smile with your eyes. How do you do that?

A while ago, we saw a television show about Richard Gere, the actor and humanitarian. He suggested something that really struck a chord with us: To each person that you meet, silently say: "I wish you happiness." It is so simple, yet so powerful.

This is how to do it: Looking at the person, smile, at the same time thinking with intent, "I wish you happiness," and without pause, continue on your way. Your wish for her happiness will move your smile into your eyes.

It takes just a moment, but this combination of acting, smiling, and wishing happiness is sure to serve several purposes. You will receive positive feedback from many of the people you en-counter. You will slightly brighten their day, even though they probably will not be aware that you were the cause. You will be-come a little happier yourself. You will realize that you are able to act (putting feeling into your thought).

Some folks may be surprised and think you are strange, so be prepared for that too!

After a while, you will not be acting the thought. The feeling will become real. It is another good habit to cultivate with ben-efits for you and for all those other people you see. Family and friends will be more responsive to you too.

Once you feel more comfortable, extend your acting a bit. If you used to feel self-conscious walking into a room full of people, next time just before you walk in, imagine how good it would feel to be perfectly poised and comfortable there, knowing that you have as much right to enjoy it as anyone else. Then pretend that you feel you belong there, and walk in as if you were full of confidence. You soon will be.

Expand this "acting" and you will soon find that your act has become your reality, with the resulting increase in confidence and general well-being. You can use this "act it, then become it" technique to overcome any obstacle where your mind has cre-ated a hurdle.

It Is Not Magic

Pretending is a very useful mind trick to use, but obviously there are limits, situations where it will not work. This technique is not an alternative to doing the work.

If you are nervous about an impending examination and fear that your nerves will reduce your performance, acting provides a useful boost. Acting as if you are able to study effectively before the examination, will also be helpful. But acting as if you know everything without putting in the work required to study and memorize, will *not* work!

You will not be able to perform open-heart surgery without training just because you act as though you can.

∾

Think of situations in your own life that you could improve by using this technique. It works particularly well with confidence related issues. For a moment, imagine that you are easily able to accomplish whatever it is your mind tells you is difficult, embarrassing, or scary for you.

· 34 ·

THE JOY OF GIVING

Resources And Value

How do you feel about giving? Do you get a thrill out of giving money, things or your time? If you have practiced wishing happiness to people you encounter (as described in the last chapter) you have already been giving. Giving happiness may be the greatest gift one can give.

Since the end of the Second World War, our society has been going through a period of ever increasing affluence. An era where succeeding generations are seeing a level of wealth and comfort their forebears would have dismissed as decadent. A by-product of this growth in consumerism is the (sometimes subconscious) belief that the accumulation of money and things is a yardstick to measure our worth. It is a fairly safe bet that either you, or somebody close to you, is a compulsive hoarder, with a basement, garage, or closets full of things that are no longer of any practical use.

Increasingly in more recent times, another sign of our worth is the appearance of being very, very busy. There may be a study that has been conducted on the subject, but merely from personal observation, it seems that we are all so busy that there is just not enough time to get anything done in a day. If you fall into this camp, ask yourself: "Am I so busy because there is so much for me to do, or is it because I make work for myself to fill up the time?"

The odds are that your answer to that question would be some variation on there being so much to do, and so little time to do it.

> Back in the Eighties, I was the Factory Cost Controller for a manufacturing company. It is my nature to be dedicated to the work I do, so I threw myself into the job. It got to a point that I was working almost every evening at home, often until midnight or later. Melanie had to beg me to take off a Saturday or Sunday to do chores around the house or go out somewhere or other.
>
> I mentioned the hours I had to work to my superior. He told me that it should be possible to complete everything that was required of me within normal office hours. He went on to instruct me not to work those extra hours any more. He said that I would still manage to do everything I had to do during normal office hours.
>
> Not believing this was possible; I reluctantly agreed to give it a try. To my surprise, guess what? He was right!
>
> This was an important lesson. Observing how my subordinates and colleagues worked, I realized that we are seldom as busy as we believe ourselves to be.

There are many reasons for us to spread work or a pastime so that it consumes all the available time, but it usually boils down to using a comfort zone to distract us from something that we prefer not to face. We have already spoken about feelings and distraction, and we will expand on that later.

Clear Out The Clutter

Getting back to giving, time used to be the one thing that was relatively easy for people to give; they had a fair amount of free time, and little else. Today, if we give, it is usually cash because our time is a scarce resource.

After reading through the first parts of this book, you realize that giving is one of the essentials for true happiness. We are taught by our religions that it is better to give than to receive. Some faiths reject ownership of anything. Regardless of any of these beliefs and philosophies, or perhaps it is because of them, the act of giving has significant psychological benefits for the giver.

Going through your closets every year or so to clear out whatever clothes no longer fit, or things that are not fashionable any more, and taking them to the local Salvation Army, homeless shelter, or Goodwill store can be very rewarding. The folks there will be extremely grateful for whatever you donate. If you are one of the many who hang onto things for no good reason ("It might fit me next year...") try it. See how good you feel. Make a note in your diary to clear out all your "stuff" again in a year's time.

This is a win-win deal, and that is a perfect outcome in any situation. And you also end up with more storage space to put all the new stuff you accumulate before the next clean out. Maybe you can get your car into the garage again for a while!

Next, go through all the other things that have been stashed somewhere out of sight and will never be used again. Recycling is good! Find an organization that can use it all. Forget about a garage sale that will bring in a few bucks that you don't need; rather give those outgrown toys to underprivileged kids.

Stop now, and mentally go through every room and closet in your home. What do you have that you cannot justify keeping?

Valuing Gifts

It is good to get into the habit of giving. Many people set up a regular deduction from their bank account to help fund causes and organizations that appeal to them. This is a worthy method of giving, particularly if you are really very busy. This way, you won't forget.

There are many levels of giving. At one end of the scale, we have Bill and Melinda Gates who are considered the greatest philanthropists on Earth through their Bill and Melinda Gates Foundation. At the other end of the scale, we have the poor unknown people who help others with the only things they have to give: time and compassion. Which giving is better or more worthy? Who knows, and does it really matter?

It seems logical that if you actually *feel* the price of the gift you give, it must be intrinsically more worthy: like the unemployed women looking after AIDS orphans in Third World countries, but the impact they will have on the planet is tiny compared to the thirty billion dollars the Gates' have at their disposal.

All giving is good, but the best giving is when you feel the cost. Even giving for the wrong reasons (perhaps just to receive praise) is undoubtedly better than not giving at all.

How To Give

Anonymous giving can provide an extra thrill. This is perhaps the purest form of giving because there is no tangible reward. Knowing that you are the only one who knows about your generosity can be pretty neat.

Every charitable organization requires funding, and donations of money are always welcomed, but one of the more satisfying ways to give, looking at it from a selfish point of view, is to donate time—working directly with the recipients of your aid. Meeting and working with those who are ill, dying, hungry, or homeless really brings it home how much we really have to be thankful for, besides being of immense help in the community.

The suggestion here is to look again at your time and budget. See where and what you can do in the community to help those less fortunate. Pick a cause that interests you, whether it is for people, or animals, or the environment. Ultimately, you will get back far more than the price of whatever you give.

Giving Is But A Part

It would be wonderful if we could give a few dollars a month, do some of the other stuff that you have been reading about, and then live the rest of our lives pleasantly with no more headaches, stress or challenges.

Sadly this will not happen. Not unless you are more fortunate than most. It has been said that life is a training ground, with continuing trials and tribulations. We cannot avoid the curve balls of life.

Sometimes it may seem that there is someone or something deliberately trying to turn you around, to stop you making the progress you desire. Looking at these stones in the road as challenges to test your real desire is an effective way to keep yourself on track.

Once you are well on your way, feeling happy with your life, you will find that these stones in your way are more like little pebbles. They are still there, and will continue to appear, but become less and less important in the scheme of your life. The now familiar phrase: "Don't sweat the small stuff ... and remember, it's all small stuff," seems appropriate.

You may already be feeling a little this way.

There is another little known consequence of giving too—particularly anonymous giving. The more you give, the more you seem to receive; the easier life seems to flow. Whether this is a karmic function or psychological illusion or fulfillment of scriptural teaching, who knows? But it happens.

When I lived in Africa, where the level of poverty and unemployment is heart-rending, I used to get an almost perverse thrill from unobtrusively placing a bunch of coins in public places frequented by these poor people. The obligation-free nature of this exchange (I had no idea who received the money and they had no idea where it came from) had a satisfying poetic feel to it.

· 35 ·

TRUTH AND APOLOGIES

What Is True

Starting off with a question again: How do you feel about saying sorry? What about backing down from a point of view? Do you have difficulty admitting to an error of judgment? How about admitting responsibility for some infraction or other?

Relationships have been destroyed through one person refusing to apologize or admit to being (or doing) wrong. To sacrifice a relationship for anything other than a matter of principle or morality would be a pity, yet many times, we continue to proclaim that our view is correct, or that our version of a story is the "truth."

There are a few points to consider here.

When talking about truth we need to realize that in most of life, the word "truth" is subjective. It is determined by the total experience of a situation. Unlike a laboratory experiment where delicate measurements can be taken at each stage of the analysis to arrive at a definitive incontrovertible truth, the "truths" that form part of our daily lives are neither measured, nor recorded for later review. The human mind has been found to be unreliable when asked to recall facts. Even under hypnosis, facts reveal a subjective slant.

Police investigators are familiar with eyewitnesses giving conflicting interpretations of the same event, sometimes with glaring differences. Perhaps you can recall similar instances in your own past where differences of "truth" have become apparent.

Similarly, points of view and attitudes towards things are reached as a result of the total experience of your life. You just have to start talking to someone about politics, religion, or something emotive like gay marriages and abortion to realize that we all interpret things differently. People are convinced that their view is correct. You will sometimes find someone quite taken aback that you see things differently!

There are a number of reasons for clinging to our entrenched views. Pride plays a part, as does a fear of being considered irresolute. Sometimes, even when circumstances change and invalidate an opinion, we blindly and unwaveringly hold to a previously stated view.

Perhaps you are not like any of these examples; it is nevertheless very useful to understand them because it helps to understand others. In understanding that they follow a different route to arrive at their position, why should we be so determined to disallow any view other than our own?

Even in a situation where there is a matter of personal principle, it is usually possible to arrive at an agreement to differ diplomatically. Where it is not a matter of principle, it is far easier to acknowledge their view or their version of truth as a possibility.

Blame And Who Or What

Allocation of blame can be an immensely destructive action. This concept is linked to crime and punishment; however here we are not concerned with that aspect of it*.

What we are interested in is the non-judicial aspects of blame: the idea that when something goes wrong, blame has to be allocated somewhere. Fault must be found. This is apparent

---

* See Chapter 45: "On Crime And Punishment" for some initial thoughts and comments on this subject.

everywhere, in personal relationships, business, sport, politics and religion.

Some say that the concept of sin is responsible for this obsession to find fault and apportion blame. Whether this is true is interesting, but not important—maybe this reasoning, in itself, indicates a preoccupation with blame!

Surely the really important question is this: Which is more important, *who* is right, or *what* is right? The answer seems obvious. Being diverted from the issue by focusing on who to attack, rather than identifying the problem and correcting it does not make sense.

Blaming alienates and divides people. Working together to arrive at a suitable solution constructively, brings people together.

Adoption of the idea that "what" is more important than "who" requires a mental shift from the way we have been raised, but it is not difficult.

This attitude helps people to express creativity more too, because the fear of ridicule is lessened. If you are not going to have all your frailties held against you, it is far easier to admit to errors of judgment and mistakes.

Yet even in the current climate of blame, it is better to admit to shortcomings. The final outcome of covering up mistakes (besides being dishonest) is seldom the one we desire. When offered an apology, the response from an aggrieved person is seldom as bad as one expects, and often strengthens a relationship. An implied message of caring, sorrow, regrets, and honor lies beneath any apology where there is an underlying emotional attachment.

In addition to this, for the apologizer, there is a distinct feeling of a weight being lifted, a lightness that follows this type of declaration.

Give it a try with something small next time there is something for which to apologize. You will probably be surprised. When you are next on the receiving end of something where you would usually have cast blame, resist the urge to point fingers, and consciously apply your mind to *what* is right. As with all else, this is a learning process.

Do it often enough and it becomes a habit. You then become an important contributor of any discussion: a mediator or peacemaker, helping to keep the focus on the most favorable outcome.

· 36 ·

PERSONAL FREEDOM

Imposed Restrictions

How much control do you have over your life? How much freedom?

Living in an organized country and community deprives us of some freedom and control. Most of the limits placed on us are worth the cost. None of us have any real problem with them other than an occasional gripe. We have become so used to them that we consider them a part of life. You would not consider walking around your neighborhood naked, nor would you decide to build your house without complying with the necessary planning regulations, permits and so on.

We live in a democracy, and these rules are there for the benefit of the many, so (to varying degrees) we happily comply. The principle behind this acceptance of having our freedom reduced is the assumption that the government (whether national or local) will not restrict us more than is necessary for a structured, functioning society. If they were to enforce draconian laws, the electorate would remove them from office at the next election if not before. There are certainly flaws, but this is a fine system in principle and there seems to be no viable alternative at present.

Covert Propaganda

Unfortunately, there are other bodies that have just as much influence over our lives, which are not subjected to the checks and balances we demand of government. There is no intent here to discredit any organization or industry. The purpose here is to emphasize the necessity to think for ourselves and make informed decisions without blindly accepting views at face value. To be conscious of, and on the lookout for manipulation

If we were only being attacked on one or two fronts, it would be a lot simpler, but we are being subtly ambushed from all sides. It comes from the media, big business, politicians, and many other organized interest groups. There is no cause for panic, only conscious awareness.

Media, in its various and expanding guises, is the main mouthpiece for most of the attacks. It used to be that the media had two distinct purposes. One branch entertained, and the other disseminated verified, unbiased, and balanced news. Advertising was accepted in order to keep the cost to the consumer at a reasonably affordable level.

Over time these two branches merged, as entertainers became social commentators, and news hounds stopped double-checking their facts before going to air or to press, encouraging the "factualization" of nothing more than opinion. At the same time, commercial interests (overt and covert advertising) grew to become more powerful in dictating the content and focus of the media in general.

Now we have advertorials and infomercials, masquerading as news. We have formulaic subliminal messaging and strategic product placement on television and in movies. We have twenty-four hour television news and talk radio, all offering slanted opinions dressed up as news to fill their voracious formats. Advertisers' fees have grown to the point that they are essentially funding the media. This allows them to apply pressure regarding the bias that is to be included in programming. How can the average viewer, listener, or reader be expected to extract fact from supposition?

Add to this the actual advertisements. These are in our faces wherever we find ourselves. A hermit's cave in the Himalayas is about the only place that you would be able to evade the reach of advertisers. And you could be sure that if more than three or four people spent any time in the cave, the ads would soon follow.

Advertisements all tell us one thing: We would be better off in some way if we were to use the advertisers' product or service.

The implication is that we are not complete until we buy what they are selling. There is something wrong with us that their product will rectify. It is fine that on a conscious level most consumers are aware that this is nonsense, and just the way adverts are done—but the cumulative negative effect on our subconscious mind of these advertisements, telling us that we are not good enough without more or better widgets, is potentially destructive to our well-being.

A Medical Example

One last, very different example: we are programmed that when we are ill or off color, we must see the doctor. Good advice. The doctor then usually prescribes medication that we get filled and take without question or concern as to the total effect of the medication. We trust that the doctor knows what he is prescribing, fully aware of all the possible side effects.

Every single drug that we use has side effects. Often the side effects are minor and cause little, if any, discomfort.

A doctor is not able to evaluate the effectiveness of each and every possible drug for a given condition fully, after just a few minutes consultation. Unless there is some known reason the medication is contra-indicated, she will play the odds, prescribing the medication that usually works in similar situations. If there is a problem, she will move you onto the next best bet.

In arriving at their favorite treatments, doctors depend upon research documentation and case studies. We assume that some governmental or independent research group conducts these studies, but increasingly, this is not the case. The pharmaceutical companies that manufacture the drugs fund the majority of studies, either directly, through grants or other, sometimes insidious, means. Reports of interference in clinical trials and the manipulation of results* are fairly frequent, but seldom reach the mass media.

Then there are the long-term effects of medication. Antibiotics are a commonly prescribed (and over prescribed) medication. They have been effective in fighting off bacterial infections since penicillin was first used, but patients are generally ignorant of the dangers associated with them.

Frequent use of these drugs leads to a weakened immune system. It has been suggested that in most instances of antibiotics being prescribed, the body's defense mechanism would have taken care of any infection on its own; ending up more able to fight off later infections. The immune system works in a similar way to our musculature, the harder it works, the better it functions. Exercise (challenge, adversity) is essential for proper development.

Antibiotic treatment, like chemotherapy, does not discriminate when destroying "bugs," killing both good and bad. Human intestines support a delicate ecology of "bugs" that are required for proper digestion of food. Wide spectrum antibiotics are known to destroy this balance, causing a number of complaints ranging from parasitic infection to food allergies.

Choose Who Controls You

None of the examples described in this chapter are included to make you throw your hands up in hopeless despair. The sole

---

* See the New England Journal of Medicine, Volume 342, May 18, 2000: "Uneasy Alliance—Clinical Investigators and the Pharmaceutical Industry" by Thomas Bodenheimer, M.D. ; and the Editorial, "Is Academic Medicine for Sale" by Marcia Angell, M.D.

purpose is to illustrate that things are not always as they seem. You cannot believe what you read or what you see, or hear (or worse, what you assume) unless you make sure that you have enough of the story.

You cannot expect someone else to ensure that you get all the facts, either. Everyone (including you and I!) puts their own spin on the facts. The only person responsible for deciding what is true for you, is you.

The only way to control your life is to make sure that you are the one controlling what gets in and what gets out.

Freedom: Taking Command

If the idea of taking control of your life is new to you, it can be quite scary to think of letting go of other people's ideas. Luckily, this is not necessary.

All you need do is start thinking about the foundation of your beliefs. Do they stand up to scrutiny, or do you feel this way merely because an influential person you know says it is so? Why do you hold this opinion? Can you justify your conviction on your own terms? There is no deadline to this, but the sooner you start, the sooner you get your power back.

In this instance, starting is more important than finishing.

When you receive new information, try to find both supporting and contradicting information, and then decide which seems most "right" to you. From then, keep a lookout for new data that may alter the balance for or against. Always be prepared to accept new information and adjust your view accordingly—but always have a valid reason before changing your mind. As you progress, you will become more adept at this.

This is a crucial part of personal growth: the ability to reassess your views and adjust them as and when warranted. This process never ends as you learn more, become more confident, and expand your horizons. By following this process, you will always be able to explain exactly why you take a particular view, even if it is not the popular one.

Always remember that most people believing something to be true, does not necessarily make it so.

As this new skill develops, you will find that your sense of being in control of your life grows. Your sense of freedom is enhanced.

Because you know what you think, and why, you are more motivated to stand up for yourself and take action to right wrongs where appropriate, either against you, or against others. In a loving way, of course!

· 37 ·

Feeling Is Fine

Good Feelings, Bad Feelings

We earlier touched on feelings, and the distractions we devise to mask those we find unpleasant. Here we revisit this important subject*.

Good feelings tell us that we are doing something good or pleasurable. They send the message: "This is nice, keep on doing that!"

Bad feelings tell us that there is something wrong, something that is disturbing. They send the message: "I don't like this, do something to take the feeling away!"

Life would be so much better without bad feelings—but remember what we discovered about the words "good" and "bad" earlier. They are no more than judgments that we apply. There is little, if anything, that is inherently good or bad. All things are neutral. How we respond to them determines their effect on us.

As Calvin Banyan said, all feelings are good. What we call "bad" feelings, are really messengers telling us that we have some need, which is not being met. If we were to listen to the message our feelings are trying to convey, there would be a lot more

---

* Much of this section is based upon the work of Calvin D. Banyan whose excellent book "The Secret Language of Feelings" is recommended for deeper insight. Published by Banyan Publishing, Inc. It is available from www.TheSecretLanguageOfFeelings.com.

happiness. Tuning into what they are saying early in the process also makes problems easier to resolve. Once we start the cycle of distraction, repression of the causative feeling camouflages the solution.

This cycle, from the first distraction through to final depression, operates as a spiral, intensifying, while generating more and more impetus as the centrifugal force increases its pressure on our thoughts. As if in a whirlpool it becomes more and more difficult to break free as the spiral draws you on down.

It is obvious from this description that recognizing and dealing with each "feel bad" situation as soon as possible makes sense. To do this, we have to be in touch with our feelings. For many of us, this is difficult because it isn't possible to be selective about which emotions we feel. The degree of intensity to which we feel one, determines the degree of intensity to which we feel all.

As a society, we tend to suppress feelings. The stigma attached to displays of emotion (particularly for men) is slowly decreasing. Despite this, most of us still have difficulty handling emotions, whether our own or somebody else's.

Identify Feeling

The diagram opposite (which you saw earlier) depicting the "feel bad, so distract" cycle lists eight feelings that can start the cycle. Becoming aware of these emotions as soon as they occur and taking action to neutralize their destructive effect will increase overall happiness by reducing unhappiness.

There are a number of steps to satisfying the missing need. We have to identify what is wrong. The deeper we have traveled around the distraction cycle, the more difficult it is to identify this correctly. It may have buried itself in our subconscious or disguised itself as something else. Look at the list of feelings below. Which one relates best to the feeling you have? Do any of the statements over the page seem to fit the way you feel?

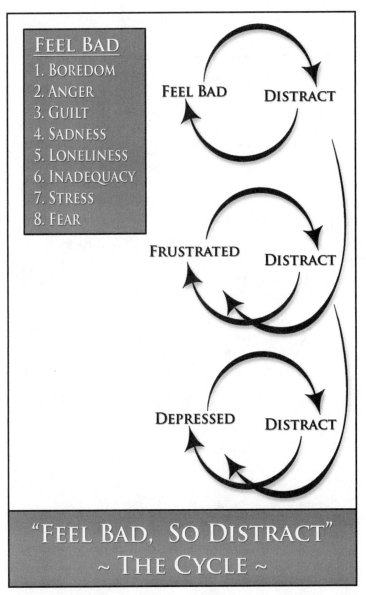

FEEL BAD
1. BOREDOM
2. ANGER
3. GUILT
4. SADNESS
5. LONELINESS
6. INADEQUACY
7. STRESS
8. FEAR

FEEL BAD → DISTRACT

FRUSTRATED → DISTRACT

DEPRESSED → DISTRACT

"FEEL BAD, SO DISTRACT"
~ THE CYCLE ~

This graphic is used with permission from Calvin D. Banyan, adapted from his book *The Secret Language of Feelings*, published by Banyan Publishing, Inc.

Boredom: *Nothing interests me.*
Anger: *Something is not right. Blame someone.*
Guilt: *I did something wrong to someone.*
   Blame myself.
Sadness: *I miss something or someone I lost.*
Loneliness: *I feel alone. Nobody cares for me.*
Inadequacy: *I cannot do it. I am not good enough.*
Stress: *I cannot cope, there is too much to do.*
Fear: *Something bad is going to happen.*

Determine Cause And Evaluate

Once you have isolated the correct feeling, look back to find the cause of the feeling. It may be a few minutes ago or many years back. Be honest with yourself. A clue to whether you have found the correct event: it will have occurred at a time before you first started your distraction cycle.

Now look at the source of why you feel so bad. Was your reaction to this cause justified? This part of the analysis is more appropriate for feelings like anger, fear, and stress, than others. Often these feelings can be more perception than fact. Is it possible that you reacted without analyzing the situation correctly? Perhaps you were too young back then to understand?

If your perception was skewed and you misread the situation, you realize there was really no reason for you to experience the bad feeling.

If, on the other hand, this is not the result of an incorrect perception, there are a number of ways that you can satisfy the need which is behind this feeling. The response will depend on the exact circumstances of the feeling involved. Each situation is different, but in short, the response is aimed at meeting the need, thereby correcting the situation.

Meet The Need

Identifying the feeling itself hints at the solution. If you are lonely, get out and meet people. Join an organization that interests you. Take steps to find someone who will care.

If you are angry, speak (calmly) to the person who angers you and explain how their behavior affects you. You may even say something like: "You have upset me by (doing whatever it is). I don't want to fight or argue about it, I just wanted you to know, because I don't want it to continue affecting me this way."

If all else fails, or if there is no other practical solution, forgive the other person as described earlier—remembering that forgiveness is for you, not the other person.

When the cause of the feeling has been addressed, your need for distraction is removed. This process will also work for new feelings, before any distracting behavior has begun.

Otherwise

If you have not satisfied the feeling, you may notice improvement but find that you only experience a temporary relief of the painful emotion, and soon it (and possibly the desire to indulge in the distraction) returns.

In this case, it is probable that the original cause of the distractions is embedded deep in our subconscious, and is difficult to locate in the conscious state.

In this case, there are several options available. You could seek professional help—certified hypnotherapists are trained to help you resolve these issues; or you could help yourself using something like Calvin Banyan's *7th Path® Self Hypnosis* program or Gary Craig's *Emotional Freedom Technique*. Both of these programs have received glowing testimonials. You can find more information on the Internet at *www.hypnosiscenter.com* and *www.emofree.com* respectively.

*All our emotional pain is caused by
our reaction to something.*

Control our reaction, and we control our pain.

· 38 ·

CHALLENGE YOURSELF

Easy Life

This is yet another habit well worth developing. It will help to keep you motivated, preventing boredom and depression.

Modern life is great. It provides all the modern conveniences to make life easier. As each year progresses, there seem to be more appliances or other aids to remove the drudgery from our lives. These inventions allow us to have more time to do the things we enjoy doing and to live an easier life.

Most of us have jobs if we want them. Even the most menial jobs pay rates that allow for a reasonable standard of living—certainly a higher standard than earlier generations. Yet it doesn't seem to bring much enjoyment.

The more conservative statistics indicate that at least one-in-five people in Canada and the United States either have, or will have some mental disorder.

Of all the mental disorders, depression is one of the most prevalent. One could debate the causes of depression but it is interesting that people who have a passionate purpose and interest in life do not seem to get depressed.

Working Purposefully

These people are all driven to achieve in whichever field they are active. Does this mean that if we all have purpose and strive to meet challenges, we will not get depressed? I am not aware of any statistics available on this, but it is my belief that this is so in most cases.

We spend the bulk of our waking hours at work. The ideal would be to have a job that you love, doing what you enjoy. Unfortunately most of us have jobs we dislike, feeling little sense of achievement when we go home for the evening.

There are fewer demands put on us to ensure our survival. For many, it takes little more than arriving for work each morning. There is little wonder that so few people feel the charge of excitement that accompanies reaching a sought after goal.

Do you feel that life just seems to go on by with little feeling of accomplishment? Perhaps you feel purposeless.

In a situation where our occupation is not stimulating, there is a temptation to perform with little or no enthusiasm, doing the bare minimum to keep the job. An alternative is to take pride in whatever you do. It does not matter whether the boss appreciates the effort put into doing a task *well* as opposed to just adequately. If you make an effort to do everything to the best of your ability, you will feel the satisfaction of a job well done. It doesn't matter whether it is masterminding a corporate business plan or scrubbing the kitchen floor.

If we refuse to accept mediocrity in ourselves regardless of the task at hand, we will feel better from within.

Challenging Recreation

A huge change, from the way things were a hundred years ago, is the fact that we have more leisure time at our disposal now. This is time that we can use up in any way we wish. You choose what you do. You can choose to spend the time relaxing, watching sport or soap operas on television, growing something in the garden or helping at an old age home.

If you feel that your life is at a loose end, you will gain purpose by deliberately taking on something that both interests you and challenges you. Learn to play a new instrument, take up astronomy, or volunteer at a soup kitchen.

∾

Life is not meant to be easy. We are meant to confront tests and grow, then confront more and grow further. We can choose some of our challenges and grow faster, or wait idly for life to throw them at us whether we like them or not.

When I was promoted to my first supervisory position at work, I was given a leaflet on business management entitled "Abdicator, Confiscator, or Delegator?" It made a great impression on me, helping to realize the qualities necessary to manage effectively. Only my subordinates over the years could tell you whether it worked!

It occurs to me that there are three similar types of individual when discussing control of our lives.

The abdicator *is the person who has given up control of her life and responsibilities. She willingly allows anyone to take charge of what she thinks. She flows with the wind, going whichever way it is blowing at that time.*

The confiscator *is the person who will take on everything. She will tell you what to think, and expect you to follow mindlessly. She has a fixed view on everything and will not contemplate the possibility of anything different. Alternative opinions are seen as a threat. She is a control freak.*

The delegator *realizes that we are all different. She knows what she believes, but investigates and assesses new facts and is prepared to change her point of view if appropriate. She happily encourages others to have their own views, seeing this as necessary for the continued growth of knowledge.*

· 39 ·

<u>Beware Of Gurus</u>

If you break your arm, your doctor will examine it, take x-rays and do whatever other tests she feels are appropriate, then set the bone and immobilize the limb. When the bone has mended, she will remove the cast, make sure that your arm is working correctly, and send you on your way.

If your car breaks down, you take it to a mechanic to have the problem diagnosed and repaired. When fixed you pay the bill and drive off, happy to be mobile again.

This process works for most areas of our lives. We need something done; we either do it ourselves, or hire an expert to help us. Sometimes, if the task is complex, it could take some time to complete the job. Once completed, you are happy and the expert moves on to her next project.

When I made the decision to spend a chunk of my life working to assist others in resolving issues and reaching their potential, there was one significant reason for selecting hypnotherapy as the main vehicle. It focuses on resolving the underlying problem, usually in a relatively short time. Other disciplines seemed to start with the presumption that treatment had to be lengthy, lasting several months or years.

You have embarked on this journey of discovery. You are learning more about yourself, taking charge of your life, and growing. It is a never-ending journey, but it is *your* journey. As you explore more, you will find yourself attracted to certain people and philosophies. This is good. But never stop asking questions, evaluating the motivation of others.

It is unfortunate that many of the people in the "self help" business seem to be more interested in snaring people, converts; convincing the gullible to believe that for them to "become," they need this guru and her latest message, book or seminar. There is always a hand out for further contributions.

For some, it appears to be a business more than a vocation. There is nothing necessarily wrong with that; we all have to make a living. This is not a suggestion to be distrustful or to stay away from those who seem to be motivated by money or fame. Indeed, they also have messages worthy of your consideration. Motivation alone does not signify the validity (or otherwise) of any position.

With the sex abuse scandal that rocked the Roman Catholic Church at the beginning of this century, many members of the church felt betrayed and started questioning their faith. These people were understandably horrified at the revelations, and by the way it was handled. Those questioning their faith were doing so because of wrongdoing by the clergy. It had little to do with the validity of the Faith itself, just abusive men of weak character.

Just as with everything else, look at the messenger as well as at the message. Saviors are few and far between. When it comes to self-development, there is no such thing as one-size-fits-all. After due consideration, accept whatever fits you and your style; reject the rest. We each have our own personality and needs. With open eyes, you can see, and then evaluate what is right for you.

Signing up for someone else's cause invariably involves subscribing to some precepts with which you do not agree. If given an all-or-nothing ultimatum, it is usually wisest to choose nothing. Be careful about making deals that water-down your principles, even by implication.

Be aware.

PART FOUR

SOME THOUGHTS AND IDEAS

Here are a few articles on diverse subjects. Some elaborate on ideas and concepts already discussed. You may notice repeated themes, such as "Chaos Theory" and the power of the mind, which always have retained my interest. These are included here despite some repetition, because they illustrate different aspects of similar things. Each article stands on its own.

These are presented for illumination and provocation. Some have been adapted from previously published pieces, others have been written specially for this book. Because stimulation is part of the motivation, your right to disagree with anything is encouraged. If you do disagree, analyze your reasons for disagreement.

Thinking about things is an enriching process. Understanding the reasons for our opinions is valuable because it helps us to accept things that are reasonable to us and discard those that are not.

Sometimes thoughts lead you where you expect, other times, not. It is always a worthwhile mental journey.

*A miracle occurs when the mechanism and rules
governing a certain occurrence are not properly
understood by those witnessing the miracle; making
the event appear to contravene the laws of nature as
they have been observed.*

· 40 ·

CHAOS, MIRACLES AND MAGIC

Isn't every kid simply blown away by magic? The pure wonder of it! We know that what we saw is impossible, but we just *saw it* with our own eyes, therefore it *must* be possible! Maybe, just maybe, I could do it too!

Of course, later when we are older, we find that the "magic" was really just an illusion, a sleight-of-hand—Misdirection. Even the great Houdini used tricks to accomplish his amazing escapes.

What about miracles? Are they also no more than a sleight-of-hand? The illusionist David Copperfield created the illusion where an entire aircraft disappears. What miracles could be more wondrous than that? Well raising the dead, maybe—especially for the person who is brought back!

History is full of miraculous stories that defy logical explanation. Science has generally dismissed these stories, labeling them as hoaxes that cannot stand up to scientific scrutiny. Repeatability is a crucial component of scientific analysis with events like these. Over the years, science has exposed many tricksters.

In religion, miracles are usually readily accepted as indisputable facts by the faithful. In each religion the deity is all-powerful, and can therefore make anything happen—and often does so (presumably) to display this power to us mortals. The performance of miraculous events is in itself often held up as a proof of the validity of the doctrine.

It could be said that one of the reasons for conflict between science and religion is due to science's need to test and analyze everything to the nth degree. Religion believes that questioning is not necessary—and is actually undesirable—as this would be questioning God (which you shouldn't have to do if your faith is strong enough).

~

I never had any trouble believing in the miracles described in the Bible, having grown up in an environment where they were accepted without question.

As we grow, however, we hear of other miraculous occurrences where the miracle may not have been proved, but can't be disproved either. Then there are all the predictions that are borne out by later events (of course there are many more that never pan out).

One of the more common miracles that we've all heard of at some point is where someone has been cured of an illness that is usually terminal, sometimes by faith healers, often not. Neither religion, nor science can explain these "miracles," although each can provide an interpretation of the events. Yet, there can be little dispute as to their veracity. Even if, as has been suggested by scientists and doctors, some of these cures are due to errors in initial diagnosis, it seems unlikely to be the cause of all these miracles. This judgment may be questioned, but it is not important.

The fact is that unexplained "miracles" seem to be performed often; and we can't explain them with established scientific methods.

The inter-dependence of all aspects of nature has been a source of wonder to me since childhood. Absolutely everything abides by a set of rules, and each relates to other parts of the delicate balance that is nature. For example, plants consume carbon dioxide and replenish the atmosphere with oxygen. These same plants run through their lifecycle, multiply, and end up providing nutrients for other plants or animals. As has been stressed countless times by environmentalists: the ecology is a delicate mechanism, which thrives when the components are in balance, and which struggles whenever the balance is upset.

So when we try to understand these miracles, predictions, and other inexplicable events it seems natural that the answer has to fit into this ordered, interconnected universe we inhabit.

As a schoolboy, I was drawn to the economy of poetry. The practice of condensing a complex idea or image into a few words with a pleasing rhythm was a discipline worth pursuing—even if nobody else understood what I was on about! One of my earlier pieces went:

everyone
knows more about something
than anyone else

Although this was written from a completely different point of view, it was a hint that pointed me in a direction to which I was later to be drawn—even before I knew it existed as a serious subject. For some time, from the composition of these few lines of poetry, my explanation of miracles was simple—if you know more about something than anyone else, you can make things happen (as if) by magic.

Without the advent of computers, this concept would possibly never have developed. "Chaos Theory" is a term that is gaining more common use, often by people with no idea to what it actually refers[*].

The most common and colorful example of chaos theory is called the "butterfly effect"—I first heard it being told by a character named Jack Weil (played by Robert Redford) in the movie

---

[*] For a description of the beginning of Chaos Theory and a different look at it, see Chapter 46: "Chaos, Karma & Spirituality".

Havana. With some variations, it explains that: "a butterfly fluttering its wings over a flower in China can set in motion a series of events which will result in a hurricane over the Caribbean."

To elaborate: A very small change at the beginning of a sequence of events can result in a completely different final outcome. A real life example is when we speak of "being in the right place at the right time"—what were the events that resulted in being exactly there at that exact moment? And then how different would things be if we hadn't been there at that precise time? What are the steps that led up to your reading this book?

You may well ask: "What does this chaos stuff have to do with miracles?"

Perhaps a lot. It means that big results can start with very small beginnings; and these small beginnings grow to become "hints," or precursors of the outcome. If we are somehow attuned to these "hints" and pick up on them before anyone else, or have the ability to sense intuitively the outcome; a prediction could appear as a miracle to someone who does not possess the same faculty.

There are many examples of this in life; one is weather forecasting. Before the advent of barometers, who would have imagined that a change in air pressure in one place would be a precursor to certain changed conditions in another place? A meteorologist taken back in time (or even transplanted into a primitive culture today) along with some of his basic instruments would be hailed as a miracle worker for accurately predicting what the weather was going to do.

Another example that comes to mind, are the fortune-tellers one sees at fairgrounds. They are adept at figuring out aspects of their customer's life by reading body language, dress, expression, picking up on bits of apparently innocuous discussion, and other (perhaps esoteric) observations. Either you or someone you know has almost certainly been blown away by the accuracy of a fortune-teller's reading.

If we think of biblical miracles, does it seem too far-fetched to believe that those highly spiritual people performing miracles could be in tune with the fluttering of the butterfly's wings?

Then, if we look at the theory from the end (from the hurricane), we know that a very little change in the course of events could cause a completely different result, so it may be possible that the final outcome could even be manipulated.

Be this as it may, the conclusion I reached all those years ago seems to be more reasonable. A person "knowing more about something than anyone else" would be able to perform (what others see as) miracles. Or to express it in a different way: a sensitive being, attuned to the inter-relationship of cause and effect may be able to divine the outcome of events, or be aware of circumstances of which we (the less sensitive) are oblivious.

We know the magic that entertains us does not really exist. The existence of miracles operating "magically" also seems unlikely when observing the functioning of nature. Perhaps emerging fragments of understanding are leading us to a more likely explanation.

> *For nothing is hidden except to be made manifest; nor*
> *is anything secret except to come to light.*
> ~ *The Holy Bible, Mark 4:22*

The need for bulk and brute strength has passed.
The need for compromise and negotiation is here.
The future demands a coordinated,
combined effort from us.

Both women and men,
sharing strengths,
bolstering weaknesses.
As equals.

· 41 ·

THE ROLE OF WOMEN:
<u>SAVIORS OF OUR FUTURE</u>

One of the people responding to the LovePeace web site a while ago, whilst commending the philosophy, expressed the view that men are responsible for the state of the world and everything wrong with society today.

You will undoubtedly have your own view as to the veracity of this opinion. Given the traditional and historical position of women in society there can be no doubt that there is at least an element of truth in the statement.

Since our ancestors lived in caves, almost every society has relegated women to a role subordinate to men. Thousands of years ago, physical strength was a requirement for survival and much like the animal world today, the strong became the leaders. Men, developed physically stronger by nature, inevitably won that role. Women and the weak were forced to bow to their strength, eventually accepting their lower status without question.

With few exceptions, the status of women was reinforced and codified in law. Until recently the bias was evident in almost every sphere of life. Our language developed full of masculine, gender specific vocabulary; laws discriminated wantonly against women; and today's major religions continue to entrench the servitude.

Throughout this time, despite all the barriers, women did not simply sit by and accept their fate as the servant of man. They developed remarkable strength and techniques that allowed them to influence all aspects of life by working in the background, negotiating, persuading, persisting, supporting, and nurturing. It was creatively subversive and extremely effective.

It is only in the past hundred years or so that women have begun to demand equal rights. Indeed, it is only in the past forty years that those rights have approached equality.

Since the beginning of the "Women's Liberation" movement of the sixties and seventies, tremendous strides have been made. Today we have women successfully running global corporations and countries—a situation unimaginable in the nineteenth century.

A start has been made. Women have undoubtedly paid a price over the centuries, and while delighted with the new freedom, some believe the achievements over the last few decades have exacted a price too. To a certain extent the effect of the feminine on society has been sacrificed in the quick rise towards equality. Probably controversial, this claim is admittedly based on subjective observation.

The natural approach to getting things done is different for women and men. Early woman achievers learnt to adapt their natural style to match that of men in order to reach and maintain their position. Adapting to the masculine methods to win their battles, women discarded some of their essentially feminine qualities. In other words, they learnt to play by men's rules, which made the victories less revolutionary. This was more palatable to the established order.

Whether running a company, a country, or a football game, the male approach to business is essentially confrontational—Gladiatorial. Challenge, aggression, and winning are essential components; sometimes submerged, but always there.

By contrast, the female leader is naturally more inclined to negotiate, persuade, and compromise. Achieving the desired objective creatively and bringing the people along as a team are more important than personal victory. Through male eyes, this approach may be perceived as weak—something to be avoided at all costs. The softer approach is confused with weakness.

History is replete with examples showing that those who rule are slow to change and will deny the evidence plain before them. Today, even with all the gains that women have enjoyed, men still rule the world. True to form, they do not see what we have done to this planet, or that change is required.

This is the stuff of revolution. It is time for women to begin a new kind of revolution. Not a bloodbath in the streets, but a gentle revolution. It is time to hold our leaders accountable to future generations. This is time for women to use their powers of negotiation and persuasion to bring about drastic change. Vote according to performance and conscience.

Both sexes have very important and valuable qualities to offer. Men have tried on their own, and failed. Women trying on their own will fail differently, but just as miserably. We are all together and need to share the responsibility to use our individual strengths to reinforce and maximize our abilities and minimize our shortcomings.

This single most important cause transcends the artificial divisions we have imagined: the survival of the species is at stake. The power of the feminine may be the last chance for humanity.

The thing about censorship and information manipulation, is that it always seems so necessary, so reasonable. The justification always measures the greater good against the alternative. Sadly, to be effective, sweeping legislation is needed to cover all eventualities.

Then when the crisis is over, the laws remain on the books and get used for purposes other than those for which they were intended.

Freedom is never free.
There is a price to be paid; and that is the price of vigilance.

Freedom has to be guarded, because the greater good is freedom itself.

· 42 ·

THE CLOSING OF THE MINDS

This essay was written shortly after the fall of apartheid and the South African democratic elections in 1994. In 1996, the Truth and Reconciliation Commission was established to help the country come to terms with its past. The horrors described to the Commission were unimaginably terrible. That people could still do these things to other humans was inconceivable.

My father was an amateur war historian who specialized in World War II. Because of his interest I had access to a lot of his reference material, and absorbed a fair amount of information about this terrible conflict.

There are a few things about the war that have fascinated me over the years. One of the most haunting revelations was the ignorance of the German people regarding Hitler's death camps. In interview after interview, I read that the good citizens were horrified to hear of the atrocities committed by their charismatic leader and his accomplices.

I could never understand how these terrors could be perpetrated without the knowledge of the general populace. Now, I understand that it is relatively easy with effective censorship and propaganda.

Even while I was having a problem believing that such ignorance could exist, the same kind of thing was happening under my nose in my own country ...and *I* didn't know!

For forty odd years, South Africa was subjected to the most severe censorship together with the propaganda that draconian censorship makes so easy.

∾

Believe me. I grew up under this oppressive system—and I thought that the rest of the world was persecuting us poor innocent South Africans. Was I wrong!

Those outside South Africa knew what was going on all the time, but the truth was kept from us. The odd atrocity that partly surfaced was conveniently written off as an isolated incident, precipitated by communist terrorists. Like Hitler, our leaders had identified the threat to the continuance of a decent life for hard working, god-fearing citizens: communist terrorists. And the government machinery continued to keep the populace in fear. These "terrorists" were the most fearful, evil, godless, rapists and plunderers one could imagine.

Most thinking people did realize that there were cracks in the reasoning and in the propaganda stories, but in the absence of balanced (or opposing) news, we simply believed in the basic good of humanity.

After all, such evil people couldn't look so normal, could they?

A true understanding of what censorship is all about is often neatly swept under the carpet by the noble appeal to protect our children; secure the national interest; preserve our Christian (or Judaic or Islamic, or Hindu, or...) way of life; or any other laudable cause that serves the interests of the Censor.

Well, of course we need to protect the children and preserve our way of life...but *we* must protect them, not the governmental bureaucracies, or the fanatics who wish to impose their narrow-minded beliefs upon all of humanity.

Government restrictions on freedom are potentially the most sinister form of censorship as they can result in tremendous power being applied to unaware citizens with little or no accountability. The initial reasons given for curbs on freedom often appear sound and appropriate to the circumstances, but the statutes stay on the books to be used later on an unsuspecting public.

If we abdicate these responsibilities and depend upon others to look after what we—or our children, for that matter—may see, hear or experience: the less freedom we will have, and our children will grow up to be nothing more than puppets.

In South Africa, a large measure of the truth has now been told. During that time the most horrific stories were daily surpassed by even more horrific and true stories.

I urge you, wherever you live, to learn from the experience of those who paid the ultimate price to win freedom from their oppressors.

Guard your freedom jealously and protect your right to know what is happening.

First published on the Internet as a component of the web site LovePeace.com: Love, Peace, Freedom, Harmony, and Happiness ~ around 1996.

Since before Galileo, there has been a running battle between science and religion. In these days when there is more freedom, religious and otherwise, there is added a similar conflict between secular and religious viewpoints.

Why is this? If God (or whatever name your culture uses) is the creator of all, surely understanding the mechanics of anything does nothing to diminish that creation? Indeed, wouldn't this knowledge enhance our sense of wonder at the complex simplicity of it all?

· 43 ·

MIND POWER VS. PRAYER

There is a tendency to separate aspects of the spiritual and the material worlds as if the other doesn't exist, providing an incomplete picture.

This is particularly noticeable when it comes to comparing the power of the mind, to the power of prayer. Asserting the power of either of these is often seen as an attack on the other, as if one can only exist in the absence of the other.

If we sit and think about it rationally, it seems that they could really be one and the same thing; merely considered from different approaches.

In the area of religion, the process by which you can make things happen (or not happen) is usually referred to as "prayer," requiring faith in a Supreme Being.

When we get into the secular field of personal (or professional) development, it is called the "power of the mind."

In philosophy, either of these views can be expounded—it merely depends upon the point of view of the philosopher. There are a number of other terms used to describe this same power, which will usually fit comfortably into either of these camps.

Religious leaders claim that the power of prayer is unlimited. The performance of miracles is cited as proof of this. If a prayer remains unanswered, or to put it differently: *is* answered but not with the desired outcome; the reason given for this is usually either that there was insufficient faith, or it simply was not God's will.

Speakers on the subject of self-development explain in a number of ways that the power of the mind is limitless. All one has to do, is concentrate, meditate in one of many ways, *will* something to happen; and it will happen. Once again, there is any number of examples of people overcoming enormous odds to achieve one thing or another by the power of the mind alone. If this will power fails to deliver the desired result, the reason given could be that the goal wasn't properly defined, or affirmations were not positive enough, or some other inconclusive fault on the part of the person attempting to harness this mind power.

Essentially, the only difference between the two approaches seems to be the agent used to achieve the desired result. In the spiritual world the agent is God, or whatever name is ascribed to the supreme deity. In the self-improvement world, the mind (or will-power) is seen as the agent.

More and more, thinking people are seeing the mind as a component of the spirit, which in turn is seen as the link to God. If we accept this, it seems reasonable to say that the power of the mind is the same as the power of prayer.

Whether there is divine intervention or not, depends upon individual belief. Those who are religious will say there is. Those who are not, will either say that there is no divine intervention, or concede that it is a possibility. In the end, it only matters in an academic sense. The mechanics are similar and the reasons for "failure" are essentially the same.

Documented results—although often unproven—from both camps are impressive, leading one to believe that (in the absence of contradictory evidence) both systems have successes.

Who wins?

Why does anyone have to win?

· 44 ·

THE HEALING MIND

The avenues that have been traveled to reach a better understanding of the mind have been so numerous they converge to resemble a highway into the brain. Yet, there is so much that is still unknown. Most importantly, we really have no idea just how powerful our brain is and where the limits lie, if in fact there are any.

The mechanics of the brain are fairly well documented. Synapses can be seen firing through a multitude of different tasks and thought processes. The areas of the brain that process certain types of data have been mapped. Even the areas that are activated during prayer and meditation have been described at length.

All this research, and we are no nearer to understanding exactly what the mind is or even where it resides, although it seems to be a function of (or in) the brain. We *think* so, anyway.

But there are so many questions still. How does perception work? Or imagination? How did Uri Geller bend all those spoons and other utensils without touching them? How much can the mind actually absorb? Is telepathy just a lucky guess? And do our minds ever fill up?

We can give ideas, opinions and supposition, but we do not really know the answers. We can put a man on the moon, but cannot explain the mind that allowed us to plan and execute the mission.

What we know about our limits, and less obvious mental abilities, is subjective, at best. There are those who believe that telepathy is just a process that has fallen into disuse as we have become more and more materially inclined. Others believe that it is total hogwash—chance, chicanery, or witchcraft. After all, there is the story of the monkeys who, if given enough time at a typewriter or computer, will eventually deliver the complete works of Shakespeare word for word.

You may be disappointed that the answers to all these questions are not going to be revealed here. But as a fellow human possessing a mind, what is more important, and far more exciting than how the mind works, is an exploration of the immense power of that mind.

It does not matter whether we can prove statistically that what we say is true. As they say, "the proof of the pudding is in the eating."

There are countless examples of the power of the mind overcoming the most daunting obstacles. Sometimes, the medium attributed to these victories is religion or faith—Divine intervention, Miracles. Sometimes the trigger is pure determination, plain and simple.

There are stories of an African witch doctor forecasting that a certain person will die on a given day. This person does not want to die, but the witch doctor predicted it (and she *is* all-knowing), so on the appointed day, the poor soul passes on.

Moving into a more familiar world; a doctor advises a patient that she has a terminal disease and only has two months to live. She dies almost exactly as predicted. Is the doctor very good, or does the patient just have the faith to believe the expert.

Young Carol has a problem with warts that seem to be popping up all over her feet. She feels tormented. Her grandmother tells Carol that she would like to buy the warts for fifty cents. Carol wants them gone, so she agrees (talk about win, win!). Grandmother pays, and says that she will come and get them that night as the little girl is sleeping. Next morning, Carol wakes up and the warts are gone. She is ecstatic!

How did grandma do it? She merely suggested that it would happen. No one can explain it scientifically but it has been known for generations that warts can easily be suggested into remission.

When you get right down to it though, there is a common denominator in all cases involving the power of the mind. There is a shift, the activation of something in the individual. A change occurs.

In the case of healing, it may be a boost in the immune system strengthening the body's defense system, an improvement in the body's efficiency to knit bones, or a reorganization of thought processes. This entity we call the mind is always the General directing the troops who storm the barricades to bring about the desired change.

If we accept this—and it seems that it must be so—we need to ask whether we actually need that trigger to reach the same beneficial goals. Could we just heal ourselves of anything, or reach some pinnacle we desire, by consciously employing the power of our mind?

The mind can put into motion the mechanism to do anything that it believes it can do, with the possible exception of defeating the laws of nature (or physics, if you are a scientist). Notice the word "possible." We do not really know all the rules of nature yet, so it is not prudent to be dogmatic on the subject.

A few decades ago, before Uri Geller took to the stage; most people would have stated categorically that it is impossible to bend eating utensils with the power of the mind. Today, the question is not *whether* it can be done, but *how* it is done.

So can we really say with absolute certainty that if Heather decided to emulate Icarus from Greek mythology, and jumped off the top of the Empire State Building she would fall to her certain death? There may be some way of doing it that we have just

206 ∞ YOUR LIFE MANUAL

not yet found. Maybe, like Uri with his spoons, Heather has the secret to human flight. For now, we consider unassisted human flight to be against the laws of nature, but in time this may also be proved wrong.

Within these ephemeral laws of nature, the mind can achieve whatever it believes it can, whether positive or negative. This belief is, essentially, faith. This faith can be in an outside agent— God, mother, father, teacher, or a pumpkin—or it could be self. Ultimately it does not matter. All that matters is the belief, the faith.

Accepting this does not mean that God, mother father, teacher or pumpkin are not important. It does not diminish their importance at all; but it does enhance the importance of belief in self. Removing the shackles of self-doubt and realizing our true ability.

Although this can be seen as a threat to anyone who is used to having power over others, it is emancipation, with potential the like of which our species has possibly never known.

∾

Here are a few things that I can attest to: things that lend credence to claims about the power of the mind over and above its everyday use. These are things that have occurred in my life, or that I have been personally involved in. I am a witness.

One: A minor exchange leads to a major life change. One day on a bus home from school when I was about fifteen, one of my friends made one of the most influential statements of my life. He told me: "You know you are always complaining about *something...*"

I was extremely shocked and upset! First, this guy was supposed to be my friend! Second, I was *not* always complaining about things. Later, at home, our exchange played over and over in my mind (the way these things do), and suddenly the realization hit me like a lightning bolt—he was right! I *did* complain a lot. From that moment, at a deep level of my being, I realized in a flash that this is no way to live life. I decided to change. My father had often told me about the "power of positive thinking" but it never meant anything before this day. I would now be more up-beat about everything.

And I have been. Finding the bright side of a situation is far more satisfying than finding the dark side.

Two: Immediately upon meeting Melanie when she was sixteen and I was twenty-two, it was plain to me that she was to be important to my life. Without going into details, after a while we became friends, and later started dating. Her parents were not too happy with this older man getting involved with their young daughter telling me one night to, "…pick someone your own age!" Some friends of hers felt that we were not a good match too, and tried to influence her to break it up. They succeeded for a while.

Knowing they were wrong, I was determined that we should be together and stay together, and patiently (sometimes) snuck into her affections. Today we are still happily married after thirty odd years. Still friends, still having fun. Did I make it happen with my mind? Who knows? But it was certainly a factor. Without that determination to woo her, I would have moved on and we would not have become the team we are today.

Three: During our studies, Melanie and I discovered Reiki, and trained to become Reiki Masters. This is a technique of healing using the laying on of hands. It is said to heal by focusing or channeling "Universal Energy" to parts of the body through the Reiki practitioner. Contrary to the belief of fundamentalists, it has nothing directly to do with religion although it does have the feel of Eastern influence, referring to *ki*, or *chi*—the life force.

From when she was young, Melanie had a cyst about the size of a marble on her head. Luckily she has a good head of hair, so it was not obvious. Doctors had said that they could remove it, but as it was not dangerous, noticeable, or painful she declined.

One day, we decided to try focusing some Reiki on it as a little test. After a few of days, the cyst disappeared and has not recurred.

Did Reiki cause this healing, or would it have healed itself on its own? Was it just a fortunate chance of timing? Once again, nobody can say, but the timing was pretty good!

After many such "healings" I believe that what happens is that the laying on of hands, through an unknown mechanism, activates and reinforces the body's defenses and that the mind unconsciously controls these functions. It is clear that a transfer of *some* kind of energy takes place. You can feel it.

Four: While I was practicing hypnotherapy, I had a young-ster of sixteen, let's call him Steve, who came to see me—he had been diagnosed as ADD. He had experienced troubles at school from the beginning. He was two years away from graduating high school if all went well, but based on his past, it did not look like this would happen. He was expected to fail. He had been on the normal pharmaceutical drugs, but this just made him feel less than alive and did not improve his school performance.

In South Africa, achieving a passing grade is largely deter-mined by taking year-end examinations that test the retention of facts learnt during the year. Steve was having trouble with both the so-called "learning subjects" (like Geography) and languages (at least two languages were mandatory).

Steve was very motivated—he desperately wanted to break free. Over a few sessions using light hypnosis and a process called Emotional Freedom Technique, with booster sessions near exam time, Steve consistently improved his results so that he success-fully completed his final examinations, graduating and obtaining entrance to the college of his choice to begin his chosen career.

This in itself was a great achievement, but Steve's attitude to-wards life was an added inspiration. He changed from being shy and withdrawn, to becoming a confident young man.

So what happened to Steve? His subconscious was motivated to make the changes necessary to allow him to believe that he could do what he had believed impossible. The ADD label, repeated failures, and the conviction of others that he was not capable had the force of a self-fulfilling prophecy on him. Then his mind, activated, turned him around and allowed him to flourish.

∼

In each of these very different examples, the mind was convinced that a change was required. It accepted the need for change, and directed the necessary alterations to occur.

Our minds are more powerful than any of us believe. This power lies dormant until called on to perform. It can kick-in to help or hurt depending on what is expected of it.

You can decide what you want to achieve, and get it.
Try it.

In a society where criminals are
afforded the same or more rights than
the population they prey upon,
only one result can be expected:
more crime, lawlessness,
and anarchy

· 45 ·

ON CRIME AND PUNISHMENT

In arriving at the philosophy described in this book, and wondering whether a whole country, or the entire planet could ever universally accept it, the likelihood that some people would not subscribe to the concepts had to be accepted—even if (in a perfect world) it was merely during a transitional period. What follows are thoughts that came out of this contemplation.
They are not suggested as a solution to "the crime problem." They are merely thoughts; some possibilities included here to stimulate your thoughts.

The philosophy of Love, Peace, Freedom, Harmony, and Happiness has the ideal of eliminating crime through its universal adoption. Given our history however, it is impractical to expect that humanity in its entirety would agree on any particular philosophy.

Even if universal acceptance were ultimately achieved, there would be a period during which some subscribe to the concepts and others resist them. Because of this, crime will not just come to an end overnight.

Additionally, we have to accept that even though there could be a reduction in "mental illness" through improved self-esteem, there will always be people who are mentally unstable and possibly prone to violence and anti-social behavior.

These realities present a real dilemma. We cannot realistically expect to live in a crime-free utopia, so how do we counter crime within the concepts of the philosophy?

These ideas will probably surprise the more liberal reader. Bear in mind that each suggestion has purpose. They are not offered as the only solution, and certainly not as the best. Look at them more as a starting point, ideas in a discussion. These ideas refer more to serious criminal behavior than the legal problems in which normally law-abiding citizens sometimes find themselves embroiled.

First, the purpose of the judicial system has to be defined. Is its purpose to punish criminals for their misdeeds, rehabilitate them, reduce crime, or merely keep them away from the population for a period?

A crime-free society has to be the ideal—with drastically reduced crime levels as the more realistic objective. Anything less would be counter productive and hinder the expansion of the philosophy.

The judicial processes in the West seem to be focused on the punishment of criminals by isolating them from society for a time. There is, perhaps, a token effort to rehabilitate convicts in some cases, but this is difficult in overcrowded prisons. Interestingly, the bastion of human rights and liberty, the United States, has not only the highest numerical prison population in the world at over two million, but also the highest number per capita with about 72 prisoners per 10,000 people in prison in 2004.

In contrast, some Eastern and Middle Eastern countries have all but eliminated criminal activity through severe penalties, with legal systems based (at least in part) on Islamic law. For comparison, Indonesia (also with a large population, a little lower than the U.S.A.) has less than a hundred thousand prisoners with less than 4 prisoners per 10,000 people in prison in 2004.

Although there are many factors influencing these statistics, it would appear that the more draconian laws have a deterrent effect on criminals. Taking this further, it seems that the best way to reduce crime significantly is to ensure that criminals will not get away with crimes. Further, when convicted they will pay heavily for them.

Considering this suggestion together with our philosophy, there is no direct contradiction: by infringing another person's right to freedom we give up our right to freedom to the same degree. One could argue for an "eye for an eye" system on this basis, perhaps drawing the line at a "death for a death."

An alternative to that could be imprisonment with no possibility of early release, and full life imprisonment (until death) for serious crimes: murder, rape, kidnapping, armed robbery, and crimes against children. To make the time served both more of a deterrent to the convict and less of a burden on the taxpayer, work gangs could be introduced to offset the cost of accommodation. Additionally these convicts should be allowed minimal comfort such as pay, gifts, and visits from family or friends.

For violent and sexual offences, punishments that include castration or other surgical procedures to make repeat offences impossible or less likely could be considered. This idea is abhorrent to many, but protecting potential victims must be more important than the rights of a person who has not valued their own freedom or that of their victims.

In other words, life in jail for these offenders must be difficult. Not inhuman, but intentionally difficult.

For crimes where there is no direct criminal intent, such as negligent homicide, the incarceration can be less severe, but still enough to be a deterrent to negligent behavior. This culprit is less likely to repeat the offence. In these cases, an effort should be made to ensure that this type of offender does not become a hardened criminal before release—possibly by separating the "real" criminals from "accidental" criminals.

This has been the dipping of a layperson's toes in the vast judicial pond. How do you think the system should be changed?

Or is it fine as it is?

*No discovery or invention in the history
of human existence has been achieved
without asking simple questions like:*

Why?
Why not?

· 46 ·

<u>CHAOS, KARMA & SPIRITUALITY</u>

*A butterfly fluttering its wings over a flower in China
can set in motion a series of events which will result
in a hurricane over the Caribbean...*

For centuries, scientists and thinkers have been looking for a
single theory that encompasses all of nature. When we discover this "Theory of Everything," it must by definition encompass absolutely everything—both material and spiritual. Many
believe that Chaos Theory is leading us towards this single theory
of the universe.

Questioning Spirituality
Should spiritual matters and beliefs be questioned?

In terms of our spiritual lives, explanations are not generally
explored. Since our ancestors first started to wonder about the
universe and our place in it, questions regarding the how and why
have to a large extent been discouraged by religious leaders.

A compelling reason to discourage examination of the articles of faith, is the reluctance of religious leaders to lose power.
To encourage questions that cannot be answered purely by reference to holy texts is to relinquish control of the faithful. There is
also the chance that some closely held components of religious
dogma might be proved false.

Even among lay people, there are many who will take the view that we are simply not meant to understand the "mind of God," and that mysteries should remain unexplained; that the wonder of the mystery may somehow evaporate with the knowledge gained.

Mankind has already uncovered many secrets of the universe, yet knowing the process and mechanics of conception and birth does not diminish the wonder of a new life. Understanding the movement of the solar system and how it influences the phases of the moon does not stop us admiring the many faces of the moon.

If anything, a full understanding of "everything" will surely be *more* awe-inspiring to thinking people than the unknown mysteries. The power of superstition, magic, and mystery over knowledge are remnants of past ages.

Furthermore, an appreciation of the processes behind the spiritual puzzle will provide a clearer path to follow in our spiritual quest.

Surely as seekers of truth and enlightenment, we should constantly question what we see, feel, and believe. After all, could there be more than one Ultimate Truth?

If there is, we seem destined to find it. As it says in the Bible: "there is nothing hidden which will not be uncovered."

The Beginning of Chaos

We have all had times in our lives when we wonder at the circumstances that bring us to the point where a life-changing event happens (or does not happen). We all know about being in the right place at the right time. This aspect of what became known as Chaos Theory has been known for centuries; it is found in folklore and has been used effectively by storytellers ever since.

But what is Chaos Theory and where does it come from? Most of us have heard the term, but have little idea what it really means. What does it have to do with spiritual matters?

Chaos Theory has been causing excitement in scientific circles over the past thirty odd years. It is a fascinating and deep subject but we will just look into part of it, the concept of sensitive dependence. It is really pretty simple to grasp—we see it operating in our daily lives.

Edward Lorenz, a meteorologist, first wrote about chaos theory. He was running a computer program to model weather patterns in the early sixties. He found that a tiny difference in the accuracy of the numbers used to start the sequence, resulted in completely different results.

What happened is that these minute differences at the beginning had a slightly different effect on each calculation in the process. Weather modeling requires a large number of calculations that depend upon the result of earlier calculations.

The cumulative difference caused by these few small differences was enormous—each step took the result further and further away from the original final answer. This is called sensitive dependence.

Before computers, this degree of accuracy would not have been attempted. It would have been considered insignificant—but in this case it was clearly far from insignificant.

Butterfly Effect

A common example of Chaos Theory is called the "butterfly effect." With some variations, it explains that: "a butterfly fluttering its wings over a flower in China can set in motion a series of events which will result in a hurricane over the Caribbean."

In other words, as Lorenz found, a very small change at or near the beginning of a sequence of events, can result in a completely different final outcome.

Taking Chaos Theory a little further, researchers analyzing various groups of data—from cotton prices, to population growth—found that, when graphed, there were repeating patterns at various scales.

Research led to the word "fractal" being coined to describe highly complex images containing shapes that repeat themselves over and over again—usually using a computer to handle the repetitive calculations necessary to generate these images.

It was found that fractals are to be found in nature too. Snowflakes, clouds, and ferns are often cited as examples.

There are early indications that fractal patterns will be used to predict natural phenomena too, particularly disasters. Knowing more accurately where, when, and how strong an earthquake or hurricane will strike populated areas would undoubtedly help minimize the effect of these disasters.

Boids, Birds, Herds, and Fish

Branching off from this, have you ever watched a flock of birds and wondered how these creatures that are not generally renowned for brainpower, manage to fly so well together—constantly changing position, yet keeping together and on course without flying into each other?

Craig Reynolds of Los Angeles wondered. He took it a step further and developed a computer program that mimics the flocking of birds (the program calls them "boids"). In developing the program, he found that each boid requires only three basic rules in order to flock:

1. Keep a certain distance from others;
2. Match speed to the others; and
3. Move towards the centre of the flock.

Just this set of rules (or *algorithm* to use problem solving terminology) results in the seemingly complex patterns of flocking birds. Observers had previously assumed that a leader bird controlled flocks—the beauty of flocking birds certainly looks as though there is some central choreography controlling their movements. It appears that the truth is far simpler—and more appropriate for our little bird-brained friends.

These same rules also seem to apply to herding animals and schools of fish. Craig Reynolds' boid algorithm has been used with critical acclaim in a number of blockbuster movies to simulate the movement of bats, dinosaurs, wildebeest, and other creatures.

We are coming to realize that there can be pretty simple explanations for things that seem highly complex, and maybe even impossible. As with nature generally, the simplified explanations make a lot more sense than the complicated alternatives.

To take this idea a step or two further, think of the human body. We know that nature is economical, so it makes sense for our DNA to be as compact as possible. Arteries, the relative size of body parts, lung structure...the list goes on and on. Could it be that a few formulae woven into our DNA strands end up in a well proportioned human?

Spirit in the Sky?

Whatever we call the "Ruler of All Things"—God, Supreme Being, Universal Spirit—we each have our own views about this powerful entity, which is usually influenced by our spiritual upbringing.

Just what do we attribute to this Ruler? Probably the first and most common answer to this question would be the Creation of Everything that Exists. This is an all-inclusive term that, besides the obvious physical objects, includes the laws of nature, relationships, our evolutionary development, and everything else.

To illustrate a possible link where Chaos Theory ties into spiritual belief, let us select a concept common to all religions and belief systems: sin and judgment, cause and effect, or karma.

No religious texts explain in detail how karma works. Our opinion on how this reward and retribution is applied depends upon religious and spiritual belief.

Ignoring the dogma, all religions essentially teach that living a good life ultimately unites one with the Universal Spirit. Deviating from this life of good, results in some form of retribution—rebirth, hell, purgatory, etc. Furthermore, our experiences in this life are in some way influenced by our balance of debits and credits.

The Law of Karma

To illustrate that the cause and effect principle is already accepted and applies in the physical world too, an easy example to cite is Newton's third law of motion. This law says: "for every action there is an equal and opposite reaction." This could easily also be offered as a definition for the "law of karma"!

There is a fairly widely held belief that all of us are connected on a spiritual level. Many consider this collective spirituality to be the force that controls the universe—God, if you will.

This connectedness is supported by empirical evidence that humans can influence the behavior of both animate and inanimate objects without verbal or tactile communication. We have all had the experience of someone close to us thinking of a subject or past event at almost exactly the same time as we do. There are stories of mothers waking up at night just before the baby starts crying, and reports of twins communicating without speaking are fairly common.

Now think back to the Chaos Theory related examples we have covered. There are simple explanations for many apparently complex problems.

Consider the idea of our DNA being coded with far more economical algorithms than previously imagined. Consider too, groups of pea-brained creatures creating flocking patterns of such beauty with just three basic rules. Then there is our psychic connection to the universe – a sensitive interdependence?

Perhaps the mechanism of karma is simply that every person is connected to every other being at a level above our current consciousness. Our intuitive sense of right, merged with that of all others, automatically measures and updates our own balance, providing the correct response at an appropriate time. At the same time, our conscience is provided with feedback, where necessary, on a conscious level.

How many DNA rules would all this take? It is well known that the human brain has far more capacity than it has ever been known to utilize. There should be no problem with us handling a few more rules—even if we are not consciously aware of it.

We could support this view by acknowledging that nature does not waste. Humans would not have a brain with greater capacity than is necessary.

The original version of this article was first published in Namasté magazine, South Africa: Volume 20, May/ June 2003 issue.

When all is said and done,
we are the product of all
our action and inaction.

The result of all our answers
to all questions.

What do you want?

Afterword

With all books aimed at helping people to reach their potential, there is a final requirement. This is a decision for you, the reader, to either adopt or reject the ideas, suggestions, or lessons outlined.

In the case of this book, there are many concepts, suggestions, and ideas. Some are philosophical, others practical. Some are conventional approaches and others perhaps seem a little strange. It is my hope that some of these have struck a chord with you.

For my part, I include all of the principles into the living of my life as best I can; however we all remain human and there are lapses.

My final suggestion to you is that you adopt as much of this as you are comfortable with, then push that comfort level a little to give yourself something extra to strive for, to provide an edge. It is the striving that adds dynamic purpose to our lives.

Then adapt what you are using to match who you are. Everything in this book should be seen as a starting point: a beginning for the new you. From here, go out and find your own truth in all areas of your life.

We are here to seek and find real happiness. By doing so, we improve the world around us.

Enjoy your voyage.

Dare to be Great!

"affirmation"
Whatever the content of an affirmation,
it is essentially a statement of a positive.

Something... *is*!

Appendix A

Affirmations

You may find some of these affirmations helpful, either to use as they stand, or to see how they are composed. Feel free to mix and match, or use bits of those that suit your desire and modify as needed.

Remember to keep them positive and in the present tense.

I am confident in my ability to do the things I want to do; this confidence makes everything seem so much easier for me.

People are attracted to me. I am interesting and nice to know because I help people feel better about themselves.

I realize that by validating others, I am validating myself.

People like me because I am a good person and worthy of their affection.

I find it easy to give of my time, my possessions and myself.

Letting go of the things that used to bother me gets easier and easier.

I know that things almost never turn out as bad as we imagine they will.

I use my mind and imagination to bring about positive changes in my life.

What I do to others, I do to myself. I encourage others to care.

There is good in everything that happens to me. My mind quickly finds that good and builds on it.

I am important. I value myself.

I like to do things for others, but measure the emotional, spiritual, and material cost to me before choosing what I will do.

I know what I can control and spend time and effort on the things I can and want to affect.

I live ubuntu. *We are all connected and important to each other.*

The world around me is a reflection by my attitude.

Everybody has the right to love, peace, freedom, harmony, and happiness. I promote these rights in every way I can.

I make choices and decisions that will enhance my happiness and improve the world around me.

My life is made up of my choices. I choose wisely.

I am happy, I am healthy and I am well.

Appendix B

Suggestion List

A short list of things to help maintain focus and direction:

- Smile more.
- Do something for yourself everyday.
- Everyday do something for someone you don't know.
- Praise at least one person for something everyday.
- Give something of yourself (money, time, …) at least once a month.
- Give something, or do something where you actually feel the cost once a year
- Stop yourself from negative and self defeating thoughts and actions.
- Learn to phrase your sentences positively.
- Take responsibility for everything that happens in your life.
- Recognise the things that you cannot control and accept them!
- Wish happiness to everyone you encounter.

Books do not make the person; and wisdom is gained mainly through experience, through living. Reading books, however, provides us with the opportunity to learn, measure and evaluate alternative ideas.

BIBLIOGRAPHY

With a book such as this, it is impossible to list all the publications which have contributed to this work. The following books are a few varied titles suggested for further reading. They cover a range of subjects of interest to me; all of which have influenced my thinking in one way or another.

Some of the copies I have in my bookshelf are older editions, acquired on various continents, so the details listed here are for current North American editions where possible. Most are available from Amazon.com.

Banyan, Calvin D., *The Secret Language of Feelings*, St. Paul, Minnesota, Banyan Publishing, Inc., 2003, ISBN: 0971229058, available from www.TheSecret-LanguageOfFeelings.com.

Batchelor, Stephen, *Buddhism Without Beliefs: A Contemporary Guide to Awakening*, Riverhead Trade, 1998, ISBN: 1573226564.

De Bono, Edward, *Po: Beyond Yes and No*, International Center for Creative Thinking, 1990, ISBN: 0140137823.

Hanh, Thich Nhat, *Peace Is Every Step: The Path of Mindfulness in Everyday Life*, Bantam; Reissue edition, 1992, ISBN: 0553351397.

Harrison, Eric, *Teach Yourself To Meditate: Over 20 Exercises for Peace, Health and Clarity of Mind*, Judy Piatkus Publishers Ltd, London, 1994, ISBN: 0749913282.

Myss, Caroline, Ph.D., *Why People Don't Heal and How They Can*, Three Rivers Press, 1998, ISBN: 0609802240.

Newberg, Andrew and Eugene G. dAquili with Vince Rause, *Why God Won't Go Away: Brain Science and the Biology of Belief*, Ballantine Books, 2002, ISBN: 034544034X.

Selby, John, *Seven Masters One Path: Meditation Secrets from the World's Greatest Teachers*, HarperSanFrancisco, 2003, ISBN: 0060522518.

Thamm, Marianne-as told to, *I Have Life: Alison's Journey*, Penguin Books (South Africa), 1998, ISBN: 0140280790, available from www.alison.co.za.

Tutu, Desmond, *God Has A Dream*, Doubleday, 2004, ISBN: 0385477848.

Yogananda, Paramahansa, *Autobiography of a Yogi*, Self-Realization Fellowship Publishers, 1994, ISBN: 0876120834.

INDEX

U

V

W

X

Z

∾

WEBSITES IN THIS BOOK

I WISH

YOU

HAPPINESS

Please visit *www.RevolutionMind.com*
and sign up to receive our free daily
quotations and inspirations by e-mail.

About The Author

David Ambrose began asking questions about the inconsistencies that he saw around him as a teenager. A keen observer of human nature, he was fascinated by the process of motivation: why we do the things we do.

Having experience in fields as varied as accounting, information technology, design, counseling, alternative healing, hypnotherapy and philosophical study; David has found elements in each, to lead him closer to his understanding of the philosophy and practice of life.

With the publication of the first web site based on his philosophy for life in 1995, David discovered far greater interest in his beliefs and the reasons behind them than he expected. This philosophy now has supporters in over twenty countries.

This interest led David to being a guest on radio shows, having several articles published, speaking engagements and now writing this book.

After living through most of the apartheid era in South Africa, and witnessing the dawn of democracy there, David moved to Canada with his wife Melanie in 2004—the realization of a lifelong desire for them both. They now live in Calgary, Alberta with their two dogs, Egg and Kappy.

If you borrowed this book and would like to own your own copy; or if you would like to order another copy (or more) for yourself or friends, please ask your favorite bookstore, check an online bookseller, or visit either *www.RevolutionMind.com* or *www.YourLifeManual.com* to place an order directly with the publisher.

Your comments can be directed to the author
through the publisher by e-mail at:
info@RevolutionMind.com

Revolution Mind Publishing
Box 51113 Beddington R.P.O.
Calgary   AB   T3K 3V0
Canada

www.RevolutionMind.com — www.YourLifeManual.com